Loving the Real Israel

An educational agenda for liberal Zionism

Alex Sinclair

D0840567

Ben Yehuda Press

Teaneck, New Jersey

Published by Ben Yehuda Press
122 Ayers Court Suite 1B
Teaneck, NJ 07666

http://www.BenYehudaPress.com

Ben Yehuda Press books may be purchased for educational, business or sales promotional use. For information, please contact:
Special Markets, Ben Yehuda Press,
122 Ayers Court Suite 1B, Teaneck, NJ 07666
markets@BenYehudaPress.com

Photographs by Alex Levac copyright Alex Levac. Reprinted by permission.

ISBN13 978-1-934730-37-9

Library of Congress Cataloging-in-Publication Data

Sinclair, Alex, 1972- author.
  Loving the real Israel : an educational agenda
for liberal Zionism / Alex Sinclair.
     pages cm
  ISBN 978-1-934730-37-9
  1. Zionism. 2. Zionism--Study and teaching. 3. Zionism--History. I. Title.
  DS149.S574 2013
  320.54095694--dc23
                              2013036478

13 14 15 / 10 9 8 7 6 5 4 3 2 1   20130915

Contents

Preface and Acknowledgments

This book is an invitation to a conversation about what I believe is one of the most critical issues facing the Jewish people today: the relationship between American Jews and Israel.

I hope that it will be read by Jewish educators who want to bring their students into a relationship with Israel; by rabbis who are thinking about how to engage their congregations with Israel; and by communal policy makers who have to decide what kinds of programs and initiatives to fund.

But, to be honest, if you're reading this, I hope that you're neither an educator, a rabbi, nor a communal policy maker. I hope you're just an interested Jew, who'd like to have a relationship with Israel, but is sometimes troubled by aspects of Israeli politics and society. Maybe you'd appreciate some new ideas about what your connection with Israel could be like in this complicated world. Maybe you're trying to figure out how to talk about Israel with your friends and family, or with your kids. Maybe a co-worker has attacked Israel, and you want to formulate a response, even though you have a sneaking suspicion that part of what he says might actually be true.

This book is really intended to start a conversation within the American Jewish community. Some parts of it are quite radical, and might make you angry. Other parts of it, I hope, will speak to you deeply and will open up new ways of thinking about Israel. I hope that you'll share all those responses with your friends, family, and colleagues. I hope the book will generate conversation.

I am grateful to Larry Yudelson of Ben Yehuda Press for taking the leap of faith in publishing this book. Many of the ideas in this book have previously appeared in print elsewhere, as I've developed my thinking over the past decade or so. I would like to thank the *Journal of Jewish Education*, *Conservative Judaism*, *Haaretz*, the *Jerusalem Post*, the *Jerusalem Report*, Synagogue 3000, and the United Synagogue's *Voices of Conservative/Masorti Judaism*, for publishing earlier versions of some of this book's material. Some of the material in the book also emerged from my work for MAKOM, the Israel education think tank in the Jewish Agency. I would like to thank some of my colleagues who, over the years, have helped my thinking about Israel engagement: Jonny Ariel, Ofra Backenroth, Roberta Bell-Kligler, Scott Copeland, Robbie Gringras, Esti Moskowitz-Kalman. I would also like to thank the dozens of students at the Davidson School of Education of the Jewish Theological Seminary, who, over the past decade, whether in my classes or on the Israel programs that I ran, were guinea pigs for my ideas and the sharpest of conversation partners in helping me refine them. Finally, I would like to thank my wife, Peri. This book is dedicated to her, in eternal gratitude for her support and love as I continue to go through my own complex conversation with Israel.

At its heart, this book is about conversation. The conversation about the relationship between American Jews and Israel is one of the most crucial — and I think one of the most interesting — conversations that the Jewish people should be having right now. I hope that that this book might be a way for you, your family, and your friends, to enter that conversation, and have your say. Clear your throat, take a sip of water, and let's talk.

Introduction

The ten-minute walk from my house in Modi'in to the town mall is rather ordinary. I walk past some apartment buildings, weave through a pretty area with some park benches and flower beds, and cross the main road to enter the mall at the entrance between the pharmacy and the bank.

But stop and think what a modern miracle that walk really is! Just twenty years ago, on this spot you would have seen only rocks, dirt, weeds: a wasteland. Twenty years ago, Modi'in simply didn't exist. It's a new Israeli city that sprouted out of the wilderness, out of nothing, but now contains much more than a pharmacy and a bank: there's a train station, supermarkets, synagogues, cinemas, shops of every kind, dance studios and theaters — all the accoutrements of a modern Israeli city, enjoyed by its 80,000 inhabitants every day.

Modi'in is a microcosm of modern Israel. What has been built here, achieved here, embodied here, over the past hundred years or so, truly takes my breath away.

I live in Modi'in, Israel's newest city, and work in Jerusalem, Israel's oldest. My drive to work takes me past Jerusalem's Supreme Court, one of Israel's most architecturally incredible buildings, past the Knesset and the Israel Museum, within a few blocks of Jerusalem's wonderful Machane Yehuda market, and finally to my office itself, which is a ten-minute walk from the Old City walls. I park my car, and breathe the fresh Jerusalem air. The sun, dimmed by its winter angle, still reflects brightly off the building opposite, the inimitable golden color of Jerusalem stone. Day in, day out, it's still a magical feeling.

And there's an added thrill: That building opposite is the residence of the Prime Minister. My office is quite literally across the road. I have yet to glimpse Binyamin Netanyahu or his wife Sarah strolling among the rose bushes, but that adds an extra bit of excitement to the hint of perfume in the air.

I didn't vote for the present inhabitant of that house; indeed, there's little he does that I agree with. Yet somehow, I manage to hold those things together in my Zionist identity: enduring love tinged with deep-seated disenchantment; genuine anger tempered by the continuing magic. My love for Israel is a complicated love. And I think that's true for a lot of other young American Jews; or would be, if we gave them the option.

In recent years, many books and essays have been written about liberal American Jews who disagree with Israel's current policies. Probably the most widely-discussed of these statements have been those by Peter Beinart, in his article in the *New York Review of Books* in 2010, and his subsequent book, *The Crisis of Zionism*, in 2012. But there have been many others, before and alongside Beinart, who have given voice to or brought our attention to liberal American Jews' disenchantment or frustration with Israel: Jeremy Ben Ami, Steven M. Cohen, Donniel Hartman, and Jay Michaelson, to name but a few.

What most of these commentators and researchers have shown, beyond a reasonable doubt, is that many young Jews today are seeking a relationship with Israel that contains both commitment and critique. In surveys, they define themselves as "pro-Israel" (whatever that means), but they are often also skeptical and critical about particular Israeli policies.

Until now, nearly all of the discourse about the problem of loving Israel as a liberal American Jew has been restricted to the realms of politics and sociology. But I'm a Jewish educator. I'm interested in how we rethink education about Israel and engagement with Israel in the light of this new political and sociological reality. How we might redefine our educational and communal discourse, curricula, and programs to speak more appropriately to this new generation of Jews. That's what this book is about.

This book sets forth an argument concerning the best way to inspire the next generation to love Israel in the years ahead, even if that love may have a different form, a different color, a different shade, from the love that previous generations felt: it may need to be a new kind of love that works for young American Jews today.

This book examines what that new love is, what it looks like, what it feels like; in educational terms, the details of how to educate for an Israel engagement of complicated love, of commitment and critique.

In particular, it examines how to nurture a love for Israel while being clear-eyed about what the country is, about what it does wrong as well as what it does right.

It is written by someone who sees plenty of flaws with Israel, despite his love for the country.

You, the reader, may share my position, and may find that this book provides a conceptual framework and justification for the kind of complicated love for Israel that you have been looking for. But if you, the reader, *don't* share my position — whether you think Israel has done no wrong, or can do no wrong, or that its wrongs are best downplayed and overlooked given the circumstances — I'd like you to consider for a moment that your love for Israel may be blinding you to her flaws. That's fine; a certain amount of blindness is something we expect from love.

But for many young American Jews, blind love is no longer a viable option. Unless we find a way to contain both commitment and critique within Jewish education about Israel, we'll be in danger of offering those young Jews a zero-sum choice: Hold on to their attachment to Israel, or their critique of Israel, but not both. And if we offer them that either-or choice, I'm nervous about the option that many will select.

So how do we engender love for Israel among young American Jews despite the flaws they see? Or along with the flaws they see?

That is the question at the heart of this book.

Pillar 1: Complexity

Three typical students

When I think about the challenges of developing a complicated-but-loving relationship with Israel, I often think about three young American Jews. I'll call them Alyssa, Todd, and Rachel; they were students of mine.

Alyssa

Alyssa is a poster child for Jewish education in almost all respects. She was very involved in USY (the Conservative Movement's youth group), she teaches in her local synagogue school, and she is now a master's student in Jewish education at the Jewish Theological Seminary in New York. She's checked off all the boxes we set up for young American Jews.

But she isn't interested in Israel.

"I just don't need Israel," Alyssa tells me. "I have a rich Jewish life in every respect. I love Shabbat, I love my community, I have a great Jewish social life, and many Jewish and non-Jewish friends. I enjoy studying Jewish texts and find meaning in many of the ritual elements of Jewish life. It's not that I have anything against Israel — I just don't need it. I have a perfectly rich Jewish life without it."

Todd

Todd is a rabbinical student, studying in Israel for the year as part of his pluralist rabbinical school's training program. He is taking classes in an Israeli college and, while he enjoys the studying, he doesn't seem to talk much with his Israeli classmates.

One day, I ask him, out of interest: "Todd, whom do you feel you have more in common with — these Israelis in your class — who are, after all, fellow Jews, also studying Jewish studies — or a group of typical liberal non-Jewish Americans?" Todd looks at me as if I've come from Mars. It's an absurd question. "The American non-Jews, of course," Todd says. "I have nothing in common with these Israelis."

Rachel

Rachel is a young woman who, like Alyssa, is working towards a master's degree in Jewish education. She's a smart, thoughtful, dynamic Jewish educator-to-be. Part of her program is a three-week seminar in Israel. In an orientation session before the trip, we go over packing lists: what to bring, how many pairs of pants, and so on.

Rachel quiets down the group for an important announcement. "We shouldn't just take our own stuff. We need to take something with us from America to give to Israelis. I think we should all go and buy a few pairs of socks, and when we get to Israel, we'll give them to an organization there that gives out clothes to the poor."

I got to know Rachel, Todd and Alyssa because for many years now, as a professor of Israel education, it's been my job to help Jewish educators, rabbinical students, and future communal leaders think about their own relationship with Israel: What role is Israel going to play in your future educational, rabbinic, or communal work? What role is Israel going to play in your life?

For many young American Jews, the answer to this question is either peripheral (Alyssa), negative (Todd), or out-dated (Rachel). What's most interesting is that I'm pretty sure that all of them, if asked the standard survey question "Do you see yourself as pro-Israel?," would answer "yes." Social science statistics can hide the complexity of what's really going on.

Some recent research points to a "Birthright bump," suggesting that the increasing numbers of young Jews who have visited Israel on Birthright are leading to stronger rates of connection. If this is true, the need for a new educational approach is even more urgent. Young American Jews who go on Birthright and become enamored with Israel are not, in the medium term, going to discard their critical faculties, or stop reading the *New York Times*. The "Birthright bump" gives us a window of opportunity to work with people and help them develop a complicated love for Israel. Otherwise, at some point, they'll end up back at the either-or choice that I mentioned in the previous chapter.

Let's now start to think about what that complicated love might look like.

Baby love and adolescent love

If you have ever had a baby, you know what simple love is. Your relationship with your baby is simple. You love her and provide for her. Period.

Your relationship with your adolescent child is much more complicated. You still love him, but you sometimes disagree with him — and he with you. You try to find ways to have these disagreements become educative and nurturing, rather than debilitative and alienating. You can collaborate with him and build ideas together. You can sometimes find each other infuriating and frustrating; yet you still try to remain in loving dialogue. It's a much more complicated kind of love — and probably a much richer kind of love.

This metaphor is suggestive of many aspects of the relationship between American Jews and Israel.

Last chapter, I told the story of Rachel, who felt compelled to pack spare socks for the impoverished children of Israel.

Would she have done the same if she were traveling to Paris or London or New York City, all of which also have pockets of poverty?

Rachel's equation of Israel with charity reflects the sad fact that too often the story we tell of Israel and Zionism is simplistic, incomplete, and out of date.

From the 1950s through the 1970s, the American Jewish connection to the state of Israel was one of philanthropic and political support for a fledgling, struggling state-in-the-making; a despised but heroic David surrounded by a series of genocidal Goliaths; a refuge for the Jews ejected from the third world; a country struggling with enormous economic problems and in need of every penny from abroad that it could muster.

Social scientists Steven M. Cohen and Charles Liebman have called this the "mobilization" narrative. It was the raison d'être for American Zionism and Israel engagement. In many Israel education contexts, it still is. We're trying to get young American Jews to love Israel with simplistic "baby love."

But the mobilization narrative is no longer accurate. Today, despite its problems, Israel has one of the most impressive and modern armies in the world, its streets ring out with more cellphones per capita than America, and its shekel is one of the world's strongest currencies. Israel today faces problems, to be sure, but these are very different problems: how a Jewish capitalist country deals with increasing gaps between rich and poor; how a Jewish democratic state integrates non-Jews in its midst; how an Israeli Judaism battered by decades of secular-religious divide might recover to become an inclusive and pluralist civil religion; and how Israel, in conjunction with its neighbors, can solve the pressing ecological pitfalls faced by this highly-populated, polluted, waterless region. Most pressing of all, of course, is the conflict with the Palestinians, and any contemporary narrative of Zionism and Israel engagement must set forth a complex, clear-headed, nuanced, and non-manipulative understanding of that conflict.

Despite these problems, in the arenas of culture, economics, film, sport, thought, retail, food, wine, and more, Israel flourishes. Israel, therefore, is a society of stark contrasts, which bounces between elation and depression within the space of hours. It is a country which one minute bursts with pride and the next minute hides its face in shame. It is a country of incredible achievements and dramatic wonders, as well as frustrating failures, misguided decisions, and sometimes sheer stupidity.

Contemporary Israel contains many facets: some beautiful, some fascinating, some frustrating, some absurd, some brilliant, some awful, some funny, some inspiring, some depressing, some perplexing, some amazing, some terrible. Israel is flawed and fabulous, inspiring and infuriating, brilliant and backward.

Most of all, it's complicated.

Rather than simplify these complications, engagement with Israel must empower American Jews to understand and enter those exciting, compelling, infuriating, frustrating complications; to love Israel like one loves an adolescent child, not a baby.

Many efforts to promote Israel seek to flatten or ignore those complications.

For example, you may remember a viral email campaign some years ago, which seemed to find its way into my inbox with only slightly less regularity than the adverts for Viagra and the letters from that nice man in Nigeria who wanted to give me a million dollars.

The email offered "good news about Israel" and listed about 20 fantastic things that Israel has done or currently does. Israel has more Nobel prize winners, computers, and books published per capita than any other country; it has leading R&D plants for Intel, Motorola, and other hi-tech companies; it puts out more patents and PhDs per capita than any other country; it can juggle while riding a unicycle; and it's basically the best thing you could ever imagine.

A recent PR campaign by a Canadian Israel advocacy group called *Size Doesn't Matter* took the same tack. The campaign gained infamy because of a sexually risqué web video clip that it produced and virally disseminated. Whatever you think of the video, though, the most striking thing about this campaign is its brazen effort to highlight only the good parts of Israel. Pictures on its website are of rock concerts, beaches, and Bar Refaeli, the Israeli model, wearing a swimsuit. It lists "factoids" containing information about Israeli society that, while not incorrect, thoroughly distort the complexity of the issues raised.

These factoids portray Israel as a liberal, tolerant, open and exciting society. It's a wonderful place to be gay (it prohibits discrimination based on sexual orientation and recognizes gay marriages conducted abroad); a wonderful place to be an Arab (an Arab woman has been "Miss Israel" and Israeli Arabs serve on the Supreme Court); and a wonderful place to be a woman (Golda Meir was Prime Minister; women represent 45% of the workforce, the same as in the US).

These facts about Israel are in themselves correct, but, because of the selective omission of complicating factors, they present a deeply skewed picture of Israel. Yes, there are pockets of Israel where gay people, Arabs, and women flourish. But there are also many sectors of Israeli society where these three minority groups face prejudice, hate, and official discrimination.

To present an image of Israel as perfect and without flaws — to deny, by omission, any of the problematic elements of Israeli society — is to set up a false dichotomy — an either-or choice — that can only work against Israel in the long run.

Israel engagement must become much, much more *complex*. It must treat the relationship with Israel as a complicated, rich, sometimes frustrating one, which requires hard work in order to keep it mutually nurturing.

In other words, it's time to grow up.

Mutual responsibility

It takes two to tangle.

When a relationship grows stormy, all parties bear some of the blame. That's true when a marriage grows rough.

And it's true when the changing relationship between adolescents and their parents reaches a crisis point.

One response to the breakdown in the relationship between Diaspora Jews and Israel is to simply blame Diaspora Jews for being insufficiently Zionist or Jewish — for not caring enough. Many people in the Israel engagement world appear to hold this view and assume that the way to solve the disconnect is to focus our efforts on convincing American Jews to love Israel more. American Jewry is where the problem is, and that's where education needs to make change. Rabbi Daniel Gordis is one of the most vocal proponents of that position. "Today's students need to learn love of peoplehood no less than they need to learn Talmud," he wrote in Commentary magazine in 2011.

I agree with Gordis that there's a problem in the relationship between American Jewry and Israel. We need to help Alyssa integrate Israel more centrally into her identity, to help Todd encounter Israelis with whom he feels connected, and to help Rachel relate to Israel in more sophisticated ways.

However, Gordis assumes — as do many Israel engagement programs — that the locus of the problem is entirely within the American Jewish context and its weakening particularism. But simply telling young American Jews that they "should" feel more connection with the Jewish people and Israel is unlikely to have much effect on their emotions.

I'm going to suggest that the best approach to the problem of Israel engagement in the Diaspora is to change the question from being a "single-location problem" to a "dual-location" or "dialogical" problem.

Let me explain.

Most Israel engagement programs are rooted in one core underlying assumption. They presume that American Jewish identity and life are in some way incomplete without, or at the very least can be enriched by, a relationship with Israel and Israelis. According to this assumption, *the problem of Israel engagement is located entirely within the American Jewish context,* and it is there that the Jewish community's efforts have been focused in order to fix that problem. American Jews are brought to Israel in order to be inspired and become connected; Israelis are sent to the United States in order to educate and inspire young Americans at summer camps; and educational researchers probe the extent to which Americans do or don't feel connected to Israel.

I certainly agree — wholeheartedly! — that engagement with Israel and Israelis has the potential to enrich American Jewish identity. However, that is only half the story, and the community's exclusive focus on that single assumption explains much of the malaise in Israel engagement, and in the relationship between American Jewry and Israel.

The other half of the story is that *the problem of Israel engagement is located not just in American Jewry, but also in the Israeli context.* That's the key difference between old forms of Israel engagement and a new form of liberal Zionist Israel engagement.

Let me highlight the problem with the following story. As the director of Kesher Hadash, the Davidson School of Education of the Jewish Theological Seminary's new semester-in-Israel program, I have held many conversations and meetings with leaders of Israeli educational institutions. The comments of one senior Israeli academic are typical. Her analysis of the weaknesses in the relationship between American Jews and Israel was rooted entirely in a critique of American Jewry:

"It's such a shame that American Jews don't feel connected to Israel," she said. "Why do you think that is?" she asked me. "Is it their lack of Jewish education, the fact that they don't speak Hebrew, they prefer to assimilate and be American, not Jewish… why don't they want to have a relationship with this country?"

At no point in the conversation, however, did she pause to wonder if perhaps *Israel* played some part in the disconnect. There was no soul-searching along the lines of "what is it about *us* that has led them to disconnect?" In this professor's eyes, *the problem of Israel engagement was located entirely in the American Jewish context.* This conversation was not unique. Most conversations, education, research and writing about Israel engagement are rooted in that single-location core assumption. They are akin to the teacher who blames his students for not liking his classes, instead of wondering whether he might in some way be contributing to their lack of interest.

Israel engagement programs that, whether implicitly or explicitly, see the problem as having a "single location solution," i.e. that focus their attention only on the weaknesses of the American Jewish context, are unlikely to succeed in the long term.

I would suggest that the single-location assumption is one of the main reasons that rabbinical, cantorial, and Jewish education students who spend extended periods of time studying in programs in Israel often end up feeling ambivalent towards Israel. They are tacitly expected to buy into this core assumption, and to prepare themselves to go back to the US and "sell Israel" to their communities, whose members are not engaging with Israel as much as they "should be."

But while they are here, they experience moments of disconnect. There is no conceptual foundation that provides the space and justification for integrating that disconnect into their personal or professional identities, or into their approach to Israel engagement. They are not provided the tools to bridge the distance or to bring authenticity to their relationship to Israel, which would, in turn, translate to an ability to share that relationship with others.

As a result, Todd feels alienated from his Israeli classmates, Alyssa is happier to conduct her Jewish life without thinking about Israel, and Rachel falls back into an engagement mode that was appropriate for the 1950s but not for contemporary Israel.

Even the best recent thinking about Israel engagement does not go far enough. The felicitous and evocative phrase "hugging and wrestling," coined by my colleague Robbie Gringras, still assumes that the primary location of the problem is with American Jews and how they relate to Israel. The notion of hugging and wrestling has been an important contribution to the field; but now we need to go further, and broaden the horizons of what we mean by Israel engagement in the first place.

Liberal American Zionism must reframe the issue of connection with Israel from being a one-sided problem, in which one party simply needs to love the

other party more strongly, to being a maturing, dialogical relationship, in
which both partners have work to do in order to improve the relationship.

We need to develop a second core assumption that puts the Israeli
context on the table, and states that it too is responsible for American
Jews' weak Israel engagement. In other words: *it's not only the American*
Jewish community's fault that American Jews don't relate to Israel; it's also
Israel's fault. I'm being very careful with my language here, and I want to
stress the "not only... also" construction in the previous sentence. This
position is not a denial of the problematic elements of American Jewish
identity and education, nor of the responsibility of the American Jewish
community to look inside itself and consider whether it is doing enough
to inspire its members to take on more Jewish rituals, learn more Jewish
texts, speak more Hebrew, and explore Israeli culture.

This position's new claim is, though, that American liberal Zionism
must *also* be rooted in the consideration of Israel's part in the disconnect.

American liberal Zionist Israel engagement must change from being
a *passive* activity, wherein American Jews are expected to be inspired by
everything about Israel, to being an *active* or *activist* endeavor, wherein
commitment to Israel *qua* Israel goes along with the possibility of open,
explicit, dialogical critique of elements of Israeli society, culture, religion
and politics.

In the rest of this book, I will explore the conceptual foundations of
this new dialogical approach to Zionism and Israel engagement. I'll suggest that there are four such foundations:

* **Complexity**
* **Conversation**
* **Empowerment**
* **Politics**

So far in this book, I have suggested that there are problems with simplistic portrayals of Israel, and stressed the need to recognize the complexity of the situation. Complexity, that first foundational element of

a dynamic relationship with Israel, will underlie everything else in this book. In part two, we'll examine how 'conversation' is a key element as well.

But first, a digression into the L-word: liberal.

A liberal digression

In this book so far, I have specified, in passing, that this is a problem for "liberal" American Jews or "liberal Zionism."

Before going further, it's worth taking a moment to explain what I mean by "liberal," and why liberalism is central to the problem I am describing and the solution I will be setting forth.

The liberal position has both political and religious dimensions, which often overlap.

Political Liberalism

Politically, being liberal is usually understood to mean being more universalistic and less nationalistic, being inclined to identify with and support the rights of minority groups, being strongly interested in social justice, and tending to believe it more possible to resolve political issues through negotiations, compromise, and mutual self-interest than through the use of military force for the purpose of subjugation.

In general, young American Jews are politically and demographically liberal. The evidence can be seen in the results of the 2008 and 2012 American elections where President Barack Obama was disproportionately supported by the young (66% support for those under 30 in 2008; 60% in 2012) and the Jewish (78% in 2008 and 69% in 2012).

As political liberals, young American Jews are likely going to be concerned about how Israel treats its minorities and otherwise respects human rights.

And they're going to be more likely to believe that Israel — or any other nation — should improve itself to measure up to universal ideas of justice, rather than be honored as a country that is already exceptional.

It's worth noting that in Steven M. Cohen and Ari Kelman's oft-cited 2007 report on the alienation of young Jews from Israel, they found that those with *conservative* political leanings were more likely to express alienation from Israel than those with liberal leanings. This data has never been satisfactorily explained or understood (or replicated). In general, though, Cohen has elsewhere argued, as have other researchers, that many of the problems of Israel engagement are particularly acute for those with liberal political leanings.

Religious Liberalism

There are a broad range of beliefs and practices within the liberal Jewish world, which includes Reform, Reconstructionist, Conservative, Secular, Humanist, and pluralist/post-denominational. What these positions all have in common, and what makes them "liberal," is that they see Judaism as a phenomenon which, rather than being purely Divine, has significant human cultural, historical and sociological influences and sources. Liberal Jews reject the fundamentalist notion that the corpus of Torah and Jewish law is literally a Divinely-authored body of work. (Some Jews who self-identify as Modern Orthodox might also share that sentiment, but in general, those opinions are much harder to voice openly in Orthodox communities.)

Liberal Jews tend to give more weight to modern values such as egalitarianism, even when those values appear to clash with tradition. Of course, there's a wide diversity among the different liberal Jewish movements, and they all navigate the tension between modern values and tradition differently. But to liberal Jews, claims from Israel's national-religious settlement movement that God promised us the complete Land of Israel in the Torah simply do not resonate.

While not all American Jews are religiously liberal, the vast majority are, despite increases in the Orthodox sector's numbers over the past two decades or so. Israel engagement needs to take account of the religiously liberal nature of most young American Jews.

Conservatives and Liberal Zionism

If you're politically conservative, you're probably going to disagree with some of my discussion of the problems facing Israel engagement. If you are religiously conservative (or Orthodox), you may not like my solutions for Israel engagement, or at least not the sources of some of my ideas, since they stem from liberal Jewish theology and learning.

But assuming that you agree with my underlying premise that a strong Israel-Diaspora relationship is to be desired, don't let your being politically conservative stop you from reading this book and considering its arguments.

For one thing, most young Diaspora Jews are liberal — and whether or not you agree with their beliefs and feelings, it's critical that we find ways to engage them with Israel.

For another, I hope that one powerful message this book will leave you with is that it's possible to be avowedly liberal and intensely connected to Israel.

Before we take the next step in building up a new liberal Zionism, we're going to explore a particular liberal approach to the Bible — one that I believe has a great potential to help us think about a liberal approach to Israel.

Pillar 2: Conversation

Yair Zakovitch, Bible philosopher

Sometimes it seems as if the word "Zionism" has become the exclusive property of traditional and religious Jews, and almost a dirty word amongst the liberal.

But it hasn't always been that way.

Zionism — the idea that Jews had to accumulate political power, return to their homeland, and rule themselves — was a tremendously radical break with the longstanding religious order. It created a breed of secular Israeli Jews who were not traditionally religious or observant of Jewish ritual, but were deeply knowledgeable about and connected to Jewish sources and texts.

One of my favorite stories about this kind of secular-but-connected Israeli has as its protagonist Shulamit Aloni, the former Member of Knesset of the left-wing Meretz party and one-time Minister of Education. Aloni, an avowedly secular Israeli, was nevertheless quite at home with classical Jewish sources. In one particularly vociferous debate in the Knesset, an ultra-Orthodox MK apparently said something insulting to her.

Aloni was furious.

"How can you say that to me, one fellow Jew to another?" she railed at him. "Weren't we both standing there at Sinai together, even though it never happened?!"

Yair Zakovitch is another such Jew for whom the Bible does not have a *religious* claim on his life, yet is unquestionably a deep part of his Jewish-Israeli identity. It is also at the center of his professional identity: Zakovitch is a long-standing professor of Bible at the Hebrew University of Jerusalem, where he has held the positions of chairman of the Bible Department, head of the Institute of Jewish Studies, and dean of the Faculty of Humanities. He is also recognized as a dynamic teacher, and, while not well-known outside of Israel, is an important figure in Jewish studies within Israel.

He has a distinctive approach to the Bible which, as we'll see, suggests a powerful analogy to Israel engagement.

The central feature of Zakovitch's orientation to the discipline of Biblical studies is the notion that *the Bible is a collection of conversations and arguments between texts*. There's no such thing as a Biblical story that stands on its own; every text in the Bible is actually in a subtle or covert dialogue with other Biblical texts.

Many other Biblical scholars have noted allusions, linguistic similarities, and other literary devices that tie one story to another. Zakovitch, however, takes these literary devices and suggests that we understand them more ideologically. Texts don't allude to other texts just for pure literary artistry's sake; they do so with larger political, religious, or philosophical purposes.

Thus, when we find allusions and connections between the story of the expulsion of Hagar in Genesis 16 and various parts of the Exodus story, it's not just literary artistry: it's a larger religious message that God does punish wicked deeds, even those committed by a patriarch, and that this punishment may last several generations. The story of the birth and naming of Jacob (Genesis 25:26), which derives his name from his grabbing onto Esau's "heel," is a subtle response to other stories of Jacob, which derive his name as meaning "trickster" (for example, Jeremiah 9:3-5). And so on.

One of my favorite Biblical conversations unearthed by Zakovitch is the one between the Book of Ruth and the story in Genesis 19 about Lot and his daughters after the destruction of Sodom. There are all sorts of similarities between these two stories: Both deal with journeys after the death of young husbands, with the consequent problem of seed for the next generation; the main characters in both stories are an older man and two women; of the two women, it is the older one who initiates and plans; the climax of both stories is a night-time sexual or near-sexual liaison which takes place after the inebriation of the man; and, at the height of that climactic scene in Ruth, Boaz twice calls Ruth "my daughter" — a direct literary allusion, argues Zakovitch, to the Genesis text, which convinces the reader that we should read the two stories as in dialogue with each other.

On the surface, the conversation between these two texts is about the Moabites. The Genesis text views them as the revolting result of a drunken, incestuous sexual encounter, forever engraved in the very name "Moab" (which the text jokingly likens to "Mei-Av," "from the father"), whereas the Ruth text argues that Moabites, whatever their origins, are in fact righteous people and can even become full-fledged members of the Israelite community.

But, Zakovitch suggests, the conversation between these two texts is really about a much deeper issue. The two stories reflect a covert polemic between two religious-political schools of thought about the intermarriage and conversion of foreigners to the community of Israel. "Non-Israelites are gross and inferior and can never be part of us," argues the writer of Genesis 19. "No they're not, they can be righteous and good and we can accept them into our community," argues back the author of Ruth.

These kinds of readings are at the heart of Zakovitch's work. The Bible, seen this way, is a collection of conversations about powerful and significant religious, political, cultural and spiritual questions. "Biblical literature," he writes, "grew from an ongoing, tension-filled dialogue between different societal thinkers."

This approach to Bible forces us to rethink some commonly held assumptions about Jewish textual history. The phrase "these and these are the words of the living God" first appears in rabbinic Judaism, and so most people think that the idea of textual pluralism began in the Mishnah and Talmud.

However, once you've read Zakovitch, you realize that this position is not quite correct. While the Bible does conceal its debates to an extent, this concealment is a lock that can and should be picked by the sophisticated reader. To say that the Bible attempts to present itself as a monolithic work is only half-true. Naïve readers may believe that they are being presented with one, uncontested view; but more sophisticated readers will be able to uncover the truth:

If we only try with all our power to read between the lines and to recon-
struct the cultural context into which a story was born, our understanding of
the Biblical period's spiritual world will be enriched, and our eyes will learn
to distinguish the multitude of streams that stir beneath the surface.

Jewish textual pluralism did not begin with the Mishnah, then; it
goes back the Bible, our foundational document. *Our Jewish textual tradition began as the record of a series of conversations.*

In one essay, Zakovitch considers what the implications of his approach are for us as modern readers of the Bible:

> Readers who are not afraid of the collapse of unity, readers who are able
> to deal with a diversity of views and opinions, will listen not just to the roar
> of the main streams in Biblical thought, but also to the murmuring of the
> brooks that quietly gurgle, to the voice of deviant traditions....
>
> ....
>
> A sensitivity to the Bible's ideational richness, dialogue and struggle,
> proves how much we are of the same flesh [*basar mib'saram*] as the Biblical
> writers, how much we are like them as we think, hesitate, hold one opinion
> and then a different one.
>
> ••••
>
> The revealing of the similarity between these ancient writers' thoughts
> and actions and between our own brings us closer to the Bible and bridges
> over the vast chasm between it and us. Suddenly we come to realize that
> some of the heavy questions that we grapple with also disturbed the Biblical
> writers...

Zakovitch has turned his academic observations about the nature of
the Bible into an almost programmatic vision about Bible readers. For
Zakovitch, through paying heed to the dialogue of the Biblical writers,
we may facilitate dialogue among readers of the Bible. *The Bible is a record
of conversations about significant existential questions, and since those conversations are left open, they invite the reader into them.*

This approach to Bible becomes, then, an educational vision:

For those of us who are Bible teachers, our task is to expose students
to these fascinating and compelling Biblical conversations; once our
students have seen these conversations in the Biblical text, they will be
moved to enter the discussion and express their own opinion. "If the

writer of Genesis 19 thought this, and the author of Ruth thought that, and they completely disagreed with each other, well, what do I think?" It is a liberating perspective on the Bible: no longer is it a distant, un-touchable document, to be kept pristine and under protective glass; it is a cacophony of conversation, with different opinions flying around, urging us to add our voices to the debate.

For those of who are Israel educators, this conversational understand-ing of the Bible can serve as a template for how we approach Israel. We will see this in action in the next section.

From Zakovitch's Bible to Israel

Zakovitch's relationship with the Bible is similar to ours as liberal Diaspora Jews — and it echoes with the same tensions that haunt our relationship with Israel.

As a secular Israeli, Zakovitch finds the concept of the Bible as the authoritative religious voice of Judaism which must permeate one's actions and beliefs untenable. On the other hand, as a committed cultural Israeli, the Bible is integral to his worldview. Reading the Bible as a collection of conversations enables Zakovitch to find some of its voices more compelling than others, rather than consider it an authoritative voice that must be either accepted or rejected in its entirety. The Bible ceases to be an ultra-Orthodox monolith, telling us what we can and cannot do; instead, it becomes a meeting ground where both radical and conservative religious positions vie with each other, as they each offer their own perspectives on powerful existential questions.

As the Bible is to Zakovitch, so Israel is to me. I don't always agree with everything Israel does, just as Zakovitch doesn't agree with everything the Bible says. For him, the Bible does not speak with one voice that must be accepted or rejected; for me, neither does Israel. For him, listening to the plurality of voices within the Biblical text gives the reader a greater understanding of the dilemmas and unanswered questions with which the Biblical writers grappled; for me, listening to the plurality of voices within Israeli society helps me understand the different approaches to its dilemmas and questions.

Israel, like the Bible, is truly a cacophony of conversations, and while some of its voices might repel and alienate me, others will attract me, move me, compel me, and enrich my identity.

So too, if more American Jews could be made aware of the plurality of voices to be heard within the Israeli debate, if they can begin to attain a deep understanding of the dilemmas and questions that Israelis themselves grapple with, then they may be able to find the voice within Israel that resonates with their own. That voice may be a "brook that quietly gurgles," but it will be a quiet voice in Israel that American Jews are able to connect with and relate to.

Crucially, just as the conversational approach to the Bible ultimately requires readers to take their own places within Biblical conversations, so too a conversational approach to Israel demands that American Jews take their places in the spiritual, political, and cultural dilemmas of modern Israel. The very existence of Israel opens up conversations about Judaism and Jewishness that were simply unimaginable just a few decades ago. It is the only place on earth where Judaism and Jewishness play themselves out in a national-sovereign-public setting. Because of this, Israel opens up all sorts of powerful conversations for Jews throughout the world.

Some of these conversations are thrilling: How might Jewish values and legal traditions inform Israel's energy, healthcare, or economic policies?

Some of these conversations are depressing: How has Judaism's narrow, insular, anti-gentile streak (and that streak surely exists in our classic texts) influenced contemporary Jewish discourse and Israeli society more than the open, outward-looking streak that, while it also exists, has been marginalized?

Some of these conversations are cultural: How does the creative tension between particularism and universalism play itself out in contemporary Israeli art and music?

Israel as a conversational text opens up these questions, offers various, multi-vocal answers, and — note the dialogical approach — invites us to have our say too.

In the next chapter, we'll add this second foundation — a conversational approach to Israel — to our first foundation — complexity — and begin to see how the dialogical approach to Israel education takes shape.

Conversations

This, then, is the second step in creating a new liberal Zionist approach to Israel education and engagement. It is ***the invitation to American Jews to engage in significant, honest, constructive conversations <u>about</u> and <u>with</u> Israel and Israelis***. Putting the first two foundations together, we see that these *conversations* must relate to the *complexities* of Israel as it really is: a society that is diverse, complex, hilarious, confusing, flawed, beautiful, ugly, spiritual, messy, frustrating, enriching, misguided, moving, old and new. American liberal Zionism must be reconceived to mean the opportunity for American Jews to engage in conversations with Israel and Israelis, conversations in which Israel's flaws and problems are discussed as openly as those of American Jewry's.

A Glimpse of Practice

We'll finish this part of the book with an initial glimpse at what this approach might look like in practice (we'll look at practice in more depth later in the book). Let's take the issue that Rachel was concerned about at the beginning of this book: poverty in Israel. Rachel's relationship with Israel was influenced by the mobilization model, which uses a simplistic and one-dimensional picture of Israel's poverty to create financial commitment to Israel, but, as I have suggested, a rather shallow and outdated form of engagement with it.

How might we not *ignore* the issue of poverty in Israel but instead deal with it in a more sophisticated, complex, conversational way? What are the conversations about poverty in Israel that could help renew American liberal Zionism?

Below are some possibilities. Read them slowly and carefully. They are enormously complicated.

✳ Should we treat poor ultra-Orthodox communities differently from poor Sephardic or Ethiopian communities, since the former are poor due to their religious and lifestyle choices, whereas the latter are poor as a result of discriminatory governmental policies?

✳ Should we think about Bedouin and Druze poverty differently from general Israeli-Arab poverty, because the former communities serve in the Israeli army, whereas the latter do not?

✳ Is the worldwide Jewish community responsible for raising funds for the welfare of Arab citizens of Israel?

✳ How are questions about Israeli poverty affected by the parts of Israel that contain great wealth? What are we to make of the skyscrapers and plush offices of Ramat Gan, Israel's "silicon valley"? Or the expensive yachts moored in Herzliya harbor? Or the Israel Philharmonic Orchestra's gala events?

✳ How economically egalitarian should a Jewish state, based on Jewish values, be?

It's worth pausing now to do a short exercise.

Take one of those questions, and think about it for a few minutes. Perhaps you can even find a friend, family member, or colleague, and talk it over with him or her. What happens when you start thinking about poverty in Israel through these prisms? What does this do to the way you think about Israel and its relationship with your Jewish identity?

These kinds of questions are not just immensely complex, interesting, and generative, but, as my colleague Esti Moskovitz-Kalman pointed out to me, they are also "educative" in the sense that philosopher of education John Dewey used the term: They are likely to lead to growth and to the desire for future similar experiences. They are "more-ish." They are fascinating. They are divergent, rather than convergent; they lead in all sorts of possible directions without pre-judging the end result. They demand connection with Jewish spirituality, Jewish texts and ideas, and meaning-making. They demonstrate that the issue of poverty in Israel can be spoken about in a more serious, sophisticated, realistic, nuanced, and yet still compelling (perhaps even more compelling) way.

Finally, they are dialogical questions: They acknowledge and grapple with Israel's imperfection, and demand that the conversation-partners take a stance, express an opinion, and move towards action.

Unfortunately, these kinds of conversations don't often happen in American Jewry.

Similarly complex and compelling conversations are possible on almost any other topic one could think of in Israeli society.

We have, then, the first two foundations of our new narrative for American liberal Zionism: complexity and conversation. Next we'll explore the question that is raised by our journey so far: How do we *empower* American Jews to enter these kinds of complex conversations?

Pillar 3: Empowerment

Three philosophers

I've argued so far that engaging with Israel requires us to re-conceive what "loving Israel" means, and that it is possible to love something deeply and to offer critique because of that love, not in spite of it. Entering complex conversations about Israel is one way in which critical love can be expressed.

But love of Israel should be more than cerebral. It needs an affective component too. In this section, we're going to explore the emotional component of engagement with Israel by looking at three philosophers: two well-known 20th century Jewish thinkers — Abraham Joshua Heschel and Yeshayahu Leibowitz — along with Nel Noddings, who is less well-known in Jewish circles, but is one of the most influential contemporary philosophers of moral education. When we're done, we'll be able to synthesize a model for a relationship with Israel that is passionate and emotional, as well as analytical, and which therefore gives a rich texture to critical love.

Heschel: the Psalmist

It has been said that American Jewry has de-emphasized the notions of place and space in Judaism; if that is the case, then Heschel may be one of the major forces behind this shift in focus. Heschel, professor of mysticism for many years at the Jewish Theological Seminary in New York, professed a spiritual, God-centered approach to Judaism, stressing its theological power.

The terms that Heschel is most remembered for capture his overall approach: "radical amazement," the way that we should try to retain our sensitivity to the world's small wonders; "when I marched at Selma, my feet were praying," his focus on social activism as a central religious mode of action; and the Sabbath as "an island in time."

Heschel's Judaism is a universalist one, focusing on its meaning for our moral and spiritual lives. It has nothing to do with any particular physical place. The modern state of Israel is simply not mentioned in Heschel's great works; we do not find it in *God in Search of Man*, nor in *Man is not Alone*, nor in *Torah from Heaven*. It's just not on his radar.

Except, that is, for one remarkable book that Heschel wrote when he visited Israel right after the Six Day War in 1967. *Israel: Echo of Eternity* is the only book where Heschel discusses the physical place that is modern Israel. The book is similar in style to Heschel's other writings, full of poetic prose and grandiose language. But in *Echo of Eternity*, Heschel suddenly discovers the power of "place" in Judaism. The book is filled with breath-taking responses to modern Israel, like this description of the Kotel:

> The Wall... At first I am stunned. Then I see: a Wall of frozen tears, a cloud of sighs.
> Palimpsests, hiding books, secret names. The stones are seals.
> The Wall... The old mother crying for all of us. Stubborn, loving, waiting for redemption. The ground on which I stand is Amen. My words become echoes. All of our history is waiting here.
> .... Once you have lived a moment at the Wall, you never go away.

However, *Echo of Eternity* is in certain ways quite different from Heschel's other work. While in his other books his poetic prose is the vehicle for highly complex theological and philosophical ideas, ideas that have literally transformed the field of contemporary Jewish theology, *Echo of Eternity* is more simple. It's a romantic ode of joy:

> Jerusalem! I always try to see the inner force that emanates from you, enveloping and transcending all weariness and travel...
> This is a city never indifferent to the sky. The evenings often feel like Kol Nidre nights. Unheard music, transfiguring thoughts. Prayers are vibrant. The Sabbath finds it hard to go away... Psalms inhabit the hills, the air is hallelujah. Hidden harps. Dormant songs. (pp. 7-9)

For Heschel, the State of Israel has deep religious meaning. It is a place where Judaism's spiritual grandeur is on display, and the Jew on

Israel's soil is smitten with radical amazement at the Biblical promise being fulfilled.

Heschel's relationship with Israel is a sweeping spiritual romance, an almost-dreamlike wonder at this place of God's presence on earth. Heschel tells us that we should never be complacent about Israel and its meaning for us as modern Jews. It is indeed a miracle. It is indeed amazing.

As I go about my ordinary daily tasks in Modi'in, I hear Heschel whispering in my ear, reminding me of how amazing my life here with my family is. As I noted at the start of this book, there was nothing here 20 years ago, and now, in the place where the Maccabees fought against Hellenism, a new city has arisen, complete with synagogues and shopping malls, schools and cinemas (combinations of Judaism and Hellenism that one hopes the Maccabees would have tolerated!). Heschel reminds me not to take that for granted — to be amazed each day afresh at the wonders around me.

I have begun with Heschel because Heschel's message for American Jews who do not see Israel as important or meaningful is to remind us just how ridiculously, absurdly miraculous the place is. It's insanely miraculous. It's breath-taking. My grandma is 94. In the world in which she grew up, Hebrew was basically a dead language like Latin. Her great-grandchildren speak, dream, laugh, and, all too often, whine in fluent mother-tongue Hebrew. Folks, *this is incredible!* We take it for granted because we have grown up in a world where there is a state of Israel, where "shalom!" is painted on the flowers at the end of Disney's "It's a Small World" ride, where the Hebrew-accented English of Israeli politicians is heard on CNN and the BBC. It's not a big deal. But Heschel tells us to pause. Radical amazement. People are speaking Hebrew? Jews are buying clothes in Hebrew, watching movies in Hebrew, making love in Hebrew? In Israel, the language of the Bible and the Siddur is used to discuss healthcare policy. Radical amazement.

Hebrew is just one of the many miracles in modern Israel. Others include some breathtaking architecture, an incredible explosion of cultural and artistic creativity in music, cinema, painting, and other art forms, and bizarre but beautiful applications of Jewish texts and Jewish ideas to the realia of modern life. And there are countless other miracles. Some people might believe that these are divine miracles; I'm okay with the idea that they are human miracles, testaments to the Jewish people's willpower, creativity, and industry over the past 100 years. Israel is an amazing place. It's by no means perfect (much more on that in a couple of pages); but it's a country where miracles abound daily, on every street corner, in every moment. What an exciting privilege it is to be involved in some way with that place of miracles! If you care about Judaism and being Jewish, then even if aspects of Israel alienate or trouble you, it's still the only place in the world where we can feel radical amazement at Jewishness on such a wide, sovereign-national level.

I believe that no matter how complex, nuanced, and critical our engagement with Israel becomes, we always have to remember the romance, the religious meaning, the passion. Without passionate vision, we will never be able to answer the "Why Israel?" question satisfactorily. (For more on the "Why Israel?" question, see the epilogue to this book.) In our relationship with Israel, just as in our relationship with Judaism, we need the Psalmist. Without the Psalmist, without that feeling of grandeur, of greater meaning, of passion, Judaism and Jewish identity become dry and meaningless. Being Jewish cannot just be about a set of ritual or cultural practices. Judaism must have purpose. It must have power. It must have passion. So too our relationship with Israel must be one of purpose and passion.

Heschel's approach to Israel provides some of that purpose. For me, at least, reading Heschel is like recharging one's oxygen tanks. This is where it all happened. This is the place that drips with Jewish history. This is what we dreamed about. This is why we're here.

This leads us to the downside to miracles. The glare from their rays can blind us to the problems that lie around them. That's why Heschel alone is not enough. That's why Heschel's approach is actually almost part of the problem. One thing missing from *Echo of Eternity* is complexity.

Even Susannah Heschel, A. J. Heschel's daughter and a significant academic in her own right, seems troubled by Heschel's unalloyed approach. Her thoughtful introduction to the second edition of the book is in some ways a defense of what she appears to perceive as her father's failure to foresee the difficulties involved in his romantic approach. She makes sure to assert that her father would have been more vocal about Palestinian rights had he lived longer. She reports oral statements that he made that provide richer and more nuanced context to some segments of the book. She suggests that the mood of *Echo of Eternity* was greatly affected by her father's euphoria of the post-1967 period. All this may well be true, but her need to assert it demonstrates just how one-dimensional, how simplistic, the actual text of *Echo to Eternity* is. It as though Heschel, freshly returned from the Birthright experience, wrote an unabashedly starry-eyed blog.

For the counterbalance to Heschel, we'll look to another great 20th century Jewish theologian and philosopher: Yeshayahu Leibowitz.

Yeshayahu Leibowitz: the Prophet

Leibowitz's approach to the State of Israel is very different from that of Heschel. Leibowitz, a devoutly religious but politically ultra-dovish Israeli philosopher, was one of Israel's most infamous public intellectuals of the second half of the 20th century. Unlike Heschel, he went out of his way to deny any intrinsic religious significance to the State; for him, Israel is and must be a purely utilitarian, secular political entity. Israel is the means by which Jews may finally achieve self-determination and rule themselves, rather than being subject to gentile dominion. That is all. It's a political-sociological endeavor — an incredibly important one, to be sure — but not a religious one.

But even if the state of Israel is not a religious enterprise *per se*, but rather a political-sociological one, it nevertheless makes certain demands of the religious Jew who wishes to partake of it. Rather than have religious Judaism function in what he saw as a hypocritical and two-faced relationship with the state of Israel, Leibowitz insisted that religion be separated from the secular state in order that the halachic system might be freed to present a real alternative to secular governance.

Israel provides Jews with the trappings, power and structures of sovereignty for the first time since the beginning of Rabbinic Judaism, and Leibowitz viewed this new status as a great challenge to Diasporic halachah. For Leibowitz, Israel is a place where Jews must reinvent halachic Judaism so that it can become a framework for informing every aspect of national sovereignty, rather than a Diaspora-oriented framework for informing only personal and ritual behavior. He therefore railed against the vast majority of religious Zionist Israelis, who operate under the assumption that there will always be some non-religious Jews who can do the dirty work on Shabbat so that religious Zionists don't have to. Leibowitz thus saved his most vehement wrath for his fellow religious: Rather than criticize Jews who don't keep Shabbat, he criticized the national apparatus of Israel, and religious Zionism's complicity therein, that assumes that it's okay and even desirable for some Jews not to keep Shabbat.

I'm uncomfortable with Leibowitz's totalitarian view of halacha; but I would suggest that Leibowitz's re-imagination of halacha as a system that could speak holistically to every aspect of a national-sovereign existence can be an inspiring idea for us. It pushes us to consider how to take different understandings of Judaism and Jewish values and apply them to things that they have never been applied to before. What does a Jewish police force look like? What does a Jewish electricity company look like? What does a Jewish bus look like? What does a Jewish football team look like? What does Jewish healthcare policy look like? Writ large, what does Jewish national sovereignty look like? *Is the Jewish textual and ideational tradition up to the task of informing and infusing the civic life of a modern country?* Can Judaism be a cultural-national resource for an entire society?

When Leibowitz perceived that Israel's national institutions and leadership were failing to live up to these challenges, when they produced policies that were not in keeping with a sovereign Jewish vision, Leibowitz railed against them angrily.

Leibowitz's anger often resulted in some memorable outbursts. He called Israeli soldiers serving in Lebanon "Judeo-Nazis," prompting an enormous public outcry. Playing on the word discotheque, he attacked the religious veneration of the Western Wall (in Hebrew, "Kotel"), calling it the "diskotel," and ridiculed the Chief Rabbi of the IDF, Shlomo Goren, as a "clown blowing a shofar."[1]

The more colorful aspects of Leibowitz's anger turned him into a deeply polarizing character, some sectors of Israeli society adoring him, others dismissing or delegitimizing him. The "celebritization" of his character is perhaps unfortunate, since it sometimes obscured the powerful religious rationales that underlay his statements. He was in many ways a modern-day Biblical prophet, a contemporary Jeremiah railing against the corruption and misuse of religion by the contemporary political leadership, and warning of the self-destructive consequences of their

---

[1] Leibowitz also apparently denigrated the game of soccer, calling it "22 hooligans chasing a ball". Here, in my opinion, he goes too far.

policies. In an article written shortly after the Six-Day War, the same period that Heschel was waxing lyrical about the stones of the Kotel, Leibowitz wrote:

> Rule over the occupied territories would have social repercussions. After a few years there would be no Jewish workers or Jewish farmers. The Arabs would be the working people and the Jews the administrators, inspectors, officials and police—mainly secret police. A state ruling a hostile population of 1.5 to 2 million foreigners would necessarily become a secret-police state, with all that this implies for education, free speech, and democratic institutions. The corruption characteristic of every colonial regime would also prevail in the state of Israel. The administration would have to suppress Arab insurgency on the one hand and acquire Arab Quislings on the other. There is also good reason to fear that the Israel Defense Force, which has been until now a people's army, would, as a result of being transformed into an army of occupation, degenerate, and its commanders, who will have become military governors, resemble their colleagues in other nations.

While Leibowitz was perceived in his time as a radical left-winger, it is interesting to note that today, a majority of Israelis, including the center-right, have more or less come to accept that indefinite control over the Palestinians in the territories may not be in Israel's self-interest. (This is not to say, of course, that center-right Israelis feel comfortable with Leibowitz's vitriolic formulation of the problem or with his specific political positions.) The right-wing government of Benjamin Netanyahu, which has of late accepted, in theory at least, the principle of a Palestinian state next to Israel, has done so largely because of its recognition of the moral impossibility of retaining hold of the territories, much as Leibowitz foresaw, and railed against, forty years ago.

Like the Biblical prophets, Leibowitz leaves us with a legacy of righteous indignation that we would do well to emulate. Israel is not perfect. Israel does some things that are really, really stupid. It does some things that are really, really awful. It shouldn't do those things. For Leibowitz, and, by extension, for us, Israel should be a place where Judaism transforms itself from a set of Diasporic rituals to a sovereign societal framework inspired by Jewish values of justice and good. When it fails, it's okay to be angry. You're a Jew: you *should* feel angry. If you don't like what Israel is doing, you should be shouting with indignation about what you feel the country of the Jewish people should be doing instead. That's Leibowitz's legacy to us.

When Heschel meets Leibowitz

Both Heschel and Leibowitz were thinkers who cared deeply about Judaism. One of the interesting things about considering them side by side is that Heschel is not widely read in Israel, and Leibowitz is almost as obscure amongst American Jews.

Heschel is the quintessential *American* Jewish theologian, enormously influential in the United States on the religious and spiritual thinking of diverse segments of the Jewish community, and in non-Jewish circles too. And Leibowitz, perhaps the most *Israeli* of 20th century Israeli philosophers, extended his influence into many corners of society, partly because of his infamous stream of provocative statements.

It's fascinating to consider why Israelis aren't familiar with Heschel and American Jews aren't familiar with Leibowitz. Perhaps Israelis are so debilitated by self-critique that they have lost the ability to feel the romance. The voices of anger and frustration have drowned out the music of the Psalms. Conversely, perhaps American Jews are so busy looking for the music of the Psalms that they simply cannot feel the anger of the Prophet at Israel's mistakes.

One thing that both Heschel and Leibowitz force us to do is to stop settling for mediocrity. Read together, Heschel and Leibowitz teach us that we should not be satisfied if Israel is mediocre. That, perhaps, is the main message I take away from reading the two of them in sync. The acceptance of Israel's mediocrity is the most dangerous attitude that Israelis and American Jews share.

The sense of settling for mediocrity can be seen in many aspects of Israel's society, culture and politics. Our service culture might be rude and obnoxious, but we are no worse than the French, so that's ok. Our army may have killed civilians in airstrikes on terrorists, but so do the Americans, so that's ok. We may be a racist society, but so are the British, so that's ok. We may have a wide gap between rich and poor, but so do the Chinese, so that's ok. And on the list goes.

The juxtaposition of Heschel's romantic vision and Leibowitz's prophetic anger can prevent us from going down this path of settling for mediocrity.

Heschel keeps us dreaming; Leibowitz keeps us honest.

The strange blend of Heschel and Leibowitz presents the theological and philosophical foundations for a powerful vision of Israel engagement and sets up a critical and sophisticated picture of modern Israel. Any vision that is infused with Leibowitz's clinical and searing critique cannot be simple. Once you have internalized Leibowitz, you can no longer see Israel entirely through rose-colored spectacles. His urgent insistence on making public Israel's wrongs, no matter the cost, is breathtaking.

Just as we should be skeptical of a vision of Israel engagement that is only rooted in Heschel's one-dimensional, post-Birthright, romantic ode to joy, so too a vision of Israel engagement that is rooted only in Leibowitz is undesirable. Too much self-critique can become terribly paralyzing. Amidst the prophetic anger, amidst the urgent desperation of social critique, Heschel helps us remember the romance. Heschel helps us remember the miracles in the midst of the mud.

These ruminations return us to a word we encountered earlier in this book, one of the words that is most often bandied about in talk about Israel engagement: love.

Nel Noddings: Not love, but caring

Earlier on in this book, I suggested that we need to reconsider what we mean when we talk about "loving Israel." Instead of loving Israel as we love our babies, doing whatever it wants and needs, perhaps we need to love Israel as we love our adolescent children. This kind of love, while it remains unconditional, allows and even demands room for argument, discussion, and dialogue.

Neither the approach of Heschel nor that of Leibowitz really fits with this conception of adolescent love. On the one hand, Heschel's romantic passion looks more like teenage infatuation than love. Most parents who love their adolescent children don't go around writing poetry about them every day. Adolescent love is something deeper, more complex, more intimate, more real. On the other hand, Leibowitz's fiery anger can't work as a love that motivates change. Certainly he is passionate, certainly he is involved, certainly he is invested... but engaging with your adolescent children with Leibowitzian fury is probably not a sensible parenting approach!

In recent years, many Jewish thinkers and educators have gotten into a tangle over this need to "love" Israel. An article in *The Forward* in September 2009 by cultural commentator Jay Michaelson entitled "How I'm losing my love for Israel" was duly followed by a plethora of responses, applause, critique, and breast-beating.

In thinking about adolescent love, I have been greatly helped by Nel Noddings's term "caring." Noddings, an important feminist philosopher of education, has reflected, in a variety of books and articles stretching over several decades, on what caring might mean in educational contexts. Here is how she defines the term:

> The phenomenological analysis of caring reveals the part each participant plays. The one-caring (or carer) is first of all attentive. This attention, which I called "engrossment" in Caring (Noddings, 1984), is receptive; it receives what the cared-for is feeling and trying to express. It is not merely diagnostic, measuring the cared-for against some pre-established ideal. Rather, it opens the carer to motivational displacement. When I care, my motive energy begins to flow toward the needs and wants of the cared-for. This does not mean

that I will always approve of what the other wants, nor does it mean that I will never try to lead him or her to a better set of values, but I must take into account the feelings and desires that are actually there and respond as positively as my values and capacities allow.

What are the elements of caring as Noddings defines them, and how are they applicable to Israel engagement, in particular when it's formulated as a relational issue?

Firstly, caring requires what Noddings calls "engrossment." It's perhaps not the most felicitous of terms, which may explain why it hasn't been adopted by a wider constituency, but its meaning is clear. American Jews, we hope, will be attentive to Israel and interested in it. Just as teachers should not expect to go about their business without being attentive to who their students are, what they are thinking, and what their world is, so too American Jews should be attentive to the thoughts and desires of Israelis, to their arts and culture, and to their political and sociological realities. Caring is a key element of Israel engagement seen through the dialogical approach.

Secondly, caring requires "motivational displacement." This notion of motivational displacement is a major departure from the earlier paradigms of American Zionism. The single location paradigm, as we've noted, sees American Jewry not as the "carer" but as the "impacted": Israel exists in order to enrich and strengthen American Jewish identity (Birthright is probably the prime example of this paradigm).

Thirdly, caring doesn't mean that you have to agree with the one cared-for. You may wish to lead him or her to what you perceive as a more worthy set of values. This is clearly an important component of loving one's adolescent child.

Caring for Israel also adds another layer to what we mean by adolescent love: understanding. As we'll explore later on, many people feel highly connected to Israel but don't always have much understanding of the complex and contradictory currents roiling beneath the surface. Care, given that it flows out of engrossment, must by definition be rooted in a deep understanding of the cared-for.

Finally, care for Israel suggests a warmer, more intimate relationship with Israel than the often-ephemeral fireworks that go along with the exclamation-marked "I love Israel!" The kind of care that Noddings suggests is a deeply emotional and meaningful activity.

You might feel that "caring" has a somewhat patronizing overtone when used in the context of American Jewish relationships with Israel. But I don't think that's an accurate reading of what Noddings means by caring. Caring requires the greatest respect between the carer and the cared-for. It requires the carer to see the cared-for as an equal. Caring, as defined by Noddings, is not one of hierarchy, but one of a purer, simpler desire to be in a relationship with the other. Crucially, in terms of Israel education, I would suggest that the metaphor of caring should be used both ways: not just to describe American Jews' relationships with Israel, but also to describe Israel's relationship with American Jews. In order for the relationship to succeed, both sides must be active partners. Many of the recurring controversies over "who is a Jew?" and denominational clashes between Israel and the Diaspora would simply not have happened if Israel "cared" for the Diaspora in the way that Noddings suggests. I'll return to this theme in the next chapter, where I'll put Heschel, Leibowitz, and Noddings together, and suggest an approach to Israel education that combines all three of them.

The intervention and the angry spouse

Taken together, the passion of Heschel, the anger of Leibowitz, and the caring of Noddings provide the groundwork for the third foundation of the dialogical approach to Israel engagement: empowerment. As we learned from Noddings in the previous section, caring "does not mean that I will always approve of what the other wants, nor does it mean that I will never try to lead him or her to a better set of values." Caring opens the door to action. Caring that is combined with passion and anger *demands* action. Israel engagement as a combination of passion, anger, and caring is a highly *empowering* activity. In single-location Israel engagement, the role of the American Jew is simply to be "impacted." In dialogical Israel engagement, the American Jew's role is to feel passionate, to get angry, to care, and therefore to act.

Perhaps the best analogy to this kind of empowerment is the intervention. According to Wikipedia,

> An intervention is a deliberate process by which change is introduced into people's thoughts, feelings and behaviors. The overall objective of an intervention is to confront a person in a non-threatening way and allow them to see their self-destructive behavior, and how it affects themselves, family and friends. It usually involves several people who have prepared themselves to talk to a person who has been engaging in some sort of self-destructive behavior. In a clear and respectful way, they inform the person of factual information regarding his or her behavior and how it may have affected them.

In an intervention, the addict's family and friends empower themselves to try to help their friend change. They read out lists of the addict's activities and behaviors that have hurt them, hurt others, and hurt the addict himself. The family and friends tell the addict that they love him and care for him — and that is precisely why they are intervening.

It may be overly provocative to compare Israel to an addict needing her carers to perform an intervention. Nevertheless, whether it be the Palestinian-Israel conflict, the non-acceptance by Israel of Reform and Conservative rabbis (an issue that is still only partly-resolved, despite recent advances), or institutional racism against non-Jews within Israeli society, there are plenty of issues which do lead many American Jews to despair of Israel and its path. A single-location view of Israel engagement offers these American Jews only two ways to respond to these issues: either to sweep them under the carpet, and therefore cultivate a relationship with Israel that is simplistic and fragile; or to break off their relationship with Israel completely. The dialogical approach, inasmuch as it sees the problem located *also* within the Israeli context, empowers American liberal Zionists to express their frustration and their disappointment at Israel within a context of caring: not walking away from their relationship with Israel, but engaging Israel more directly about what they perceive as its mistakes. It's loving Israel as you love a true friend: with passion, sometimes with anger, with care.

Another analogy that may help flesh out the conceptual framework for this paradigm of active care is more Jewishly rooted, and perhaps more palatable than the intervention metaphor.

There is a famous comment by Rashi on Genesis 2:18, in which God decides to create a partner for Adam. The Biblical narrator has God say, "It is not good for man to be alone; I will make him a helper against him." The Hebrew here, "*ezer k'negdo*," is tricky and has always perplexed translators. Some try "corresponding to him," some try "beside him," some try "fitting." None of these captures the oddness of the Hebrew.

Rashi comments as follows: "If he is worthy: a helper; if he is not worthy: against him, to fight with him." Generations of rabbis have used this beautiful comment to talk about the complexity of the relationship between spouses, and to suggest that a true marriage is based on the ability and willingness to give honest and critical feedback to one's spouse if they lose their way. A spouse is not a yes-man (or woman); a spouse is someone who is empowered to disagree with you, and to tell you so, when you are wrong.

Through this comment and the beautiful, paradoxical phrase it explains, we may be able to develop a more helpful vision for a relationship between American Jewry and Israel. As 'challenging helpers,' American Jews may offer angry and vocal (although ideally also passionate and constructive) critique when they feel that Israel is practicing particular policies that they find unworthy. This critique is all the more powerful because it is a spouse's, not a stranger's.

Passion, anger, and caring, when combined, create a model of empowerment that is essential for a dialogical approach to Israel engagement. Understand Israel's complexity; listen to and get involved in its many complex conversations about compelling issues; become empowered to state your opinion in those conversation with passion, sometimes anger, and care.

Why Israel needs American voices

The paradigm of passionate angry care will help not just American Jews and their connection to Israel, but Israel itself. As a passionate Jew living in Israel, I feel that the lack of American Jewish voices in modern Israel is a grave problem. Israel, for all its wonders, its achievements, and its robustness, is not living up to its potential, and one of the reasons for that gap (I believe) is the lack of American Jewish voices in its culture, religion, and politics. American Liberal Zionism has focused over-much on how to create "impact" on its American constituency and not given enough attention to creating a forum for American voices to be heard in the complex conversations about the truly tough issues currently facing Israelis and Israeli society.

There are many voices that are already waiting to be heard, each of which has the possibility of engaging American Jews more fully while also helping Israelis to find new ways to approach their age-old issues. For example, Thomas Friedman writes as perceptively about Israeli politics as any Israeli journalist or politician; yet his pieces are seldom translated into Hebrew. How much would Israeli discourse be enriched if Israelis allowed him to express his "passionate-angry-care"? Or: Heschel revolutionized our understanding of Jewish spirituality; but as noted earlier, most religious Israelis have never heard of him. Or: How might Israel benefit by examining and learning from the ways in which American Jews of many streams acknowledge one another and learn from each other?

There are countless other examples. Both sides are at fault. Israelis have been too stubborn, too arrogant, or too busy, to listen; but American Jews have not sufficiently empowered themselves to make their voices heard.

One of the reasons that American Jews have chosen not to empower themselves to make their voices heard is a reticence to get involved in internal Israeli political issues. In the next part of the book, I'll argue that that reticence is a mistake, and that American Jews' relationships with Israel must include a full-on engagement with Israeli politics.

Pillar 4: Politics

It's all political

In the 1990s, there used to be an Israeli current affairs show on television called "It's all political" ("Hakol politi"). It was an interesting window into Israeli society and political culture. The set was a large round table, around which six to eight guests would sit, mostly politicians and journalists, and the show basically consisted of these guests shouting at each other for an hour and a half. Most of the time, as I watched it, I didn't know whether to laugh or cry: laugh, because it was really funny watching these grown men and women compete to see who could interrupt the most, talk the loudest, be the rudest; cry, because these were the people who were running the country. Oy vey.

However, I remember the show not because of its content, but because of its title. What a great title. Israeli society is indeed all politics. Every corner of Israel is loaded with political questions. In Israel, you can't get on a bus without politics. (Should I shrug my shoulders at the ultra-Orthodox attempts to gender-segregate, or should I fight against it by sitting next to a woman?) You can't go to the supermarket without politics. (Should I boycott food produced in the occupied territories, or food that has the coercive ultra-Orthodox kashrut seal on it, or food from the company that has near-monopoly control of the market? — there have been recent campaigns for all of these boycotts).

Israel is a political place. It's all politics. Israelis mark themselves off politically by the clothes they wear, by what they put or don't put on their heads, by the food they eat, by the newspapers they read, by the schools they send their children to, and by the neighborhoods they live in.

And yet, those involved professionally in 'Israel engagement' shy away from politics. We like to engage with Israel without being divisive. We like to engage with Israel without alienating people. We ask people to be "Zionist" or "Israel-engaged" without being overtly political. But it's a mistake to think that we can engage with a place without paying attention to one of that place's most significant and pervasive characteristics. Yes, it's controversial, but I believe that politics must be the fourth pillar of the dialogical Israel engagement agenda. I'll explain why, and address some of the objections to this approach. First, though, we need to look at some ideas about patriotism in general, and see how they might help us think about Zionism.

Democratic patriotism

In a fascinating article in *Phi Delta Kappan*, the educational policy magazine, Joel Westheimer, a professor of politics and education at the University of Ottawa, proposes two models of patriotism, which he calls "authoritarian patriotism" and "democratic patriotism." Authoritarian patriotism is characterized by an unquestioning loyalty to one's country which sees dissent over its policies as dangerous and destabilizing: "my country, right or wrong," as the slogan goes. Democratic patriotism, on the other hand, believes in a deliberative, critical, questioning stance towards one's country, admiring its underlying values and ideals but being respectful and even encouraging of dissent towards its perceived shortcomings.

Westheimer uses this distinction to do some compelling thinking about American reactions to the war against terrorism after 9/11, in particular criticizing certain schools for practicing an extreme form of authoritarian patriotism and leaving no room for students or teachers who saw themselves as democratic patriots. He finishes the essay with an impassioned claim for democratic patriotism:

> But a democratic public is best served by a democratic form of patriotism. To ensure the strength of our democratic institutions and to foster a democratic patriotism that is loyal to the American ideals of equality, compassion, and justice, adults must struggle with difficult policy debates in all available democratic arenas.

I find Westheimer very convincing. I often do a simple exercise in classes which makes the case for democratic patriotism. I ask students to raise their hands if they love their country (America). Everyone raises their hand. I then ask students to *keep their hands raised* if they agree with everything that Americans or the American government have ever done. All the hands come down. I then ask students to raise their hands again if they think that it's okay for them to criticize other Americans or the American government when they disagree with their policies. All the hands are raised once more. It's a great little exercise, because its visual and movement aspects make its point clearly.

That's all well and good if you're a democratic patriot living in America, talking about America. It may not always be easy to practice democratic patriotism, but it seems to be a rational and credible position.

Can we, though, extend the idea of democratic patriotism to American Jews' relationship with Israel? Can you practice democratic patriotism when you don't live in the country you're being patriotic about?

When I do the hand-raising exercise again, substituting "Israel" for "America," students become more uncertain about when to lower and raise their hands.

Can you have "Democratic Zionism"?

American voices in Israeli affairs

Both Israelis and the American Jewish communal leadership have often expressed deep reservations about what I am here calling democratic Zionism. Israelis don't like it when Diaspora Jews criticize Israel, and much of the American Jewish establishment also feels uncomfortable about "washing dirty laundry in public." In a 2010 op-ed in Haaretz, the influential Israeli political scientist Professor Shlomo Avineri gave voice to this classic paradigm of the American Jewish relationship with Israel as follows:

> I would like to note that I'm not comfortable with a situation in which people who don't live in Israel and won't be bearing the possible repercussions of the policies they advocate give themselves license to intervene in the political process here. This applies to figures on the right as well as on the left. For all of Diaspora Jewry's affinity to Israel, the tough political decisions must be ours — and ours alone — to make, and it isn't fitting for non-citizens to have any part or parcel in those decisions.
>
> That's the difference between citizenship, which entails responsibility, and support or sympathy. (*Haaretz*, May 10, 2010).

To my mind, Avineri makes three errors here, errors which are often made in discussions about Israel-Diaspora relations. Firstly, in the discourse about Israel-Diaspora relations, we don't sufficiently differentiate between the making of political decisions and the forthright expressing of opinions. Even if you believe that only citizens, who have both the rights and responsibilities of living in a sovereign, self-governing country, can actually make political decisions, that does not mitigate the right of interested parties and outside supporters to express their opinions. One of the reasons that liberal American Jews have become so alienated from Israel is that they often feel silenced, feel that there is no place in communal discourse for a "democratic Zionist" approach to Israel. A dialogical approach to Israel engagement would demand such communal discourse.

The second mistake we often make is that we ignore the fact that many internal political decisions in Israel directly affect Diaspora Jews.

If Israel is to be the "representative of the Jewish public," as Avineri puts it elsewhere in that same article, then its policies on Jewishness must be formulated in conjunction with the Jewish world and not in opposition to it. One can point to many obvious examples of Israeli policies that have been carried out without taking into account Diaspora Jewish opinion: the laws on conversion, state non-recognition of non-orthodox marriage, and the situation at the Kotel (Western Wall), which, by being placed under the control of the ultra-Orthodox, is rapidly turning Judaism's most ancient monument into one of the main forces for the disintegration of Jewish peoplehood. (At time of writing, attempts are under way to find a solution which would be acceptable to liberal Jewish groups)

While laws about Jewishness are the clearest cases where Diaspora Jewry should be allowed to (at the very least) express opinions, and, ideally, be involved in the decision-making process, we might do well to consider other policy areas too. Many Israelis reject the idea, for example, that Diaspora Jews should have anything to do with the fate of Jerusalem. But I would suggest that the views of Diaspora Jews *should* be taken into consideration when contemplating Jerusalem's future. The city has been a Jewish symbol for much longer than the State of Israel has existed. It may be that many Israeli Jews can only conceive of Jerusalem as "the eternal, undivided capital of Israel," but for many Diaspora Jews, a much more powerful and *Jewish* vision of Jerusalem would be as a beacon for tolerance and co-existence, a city which we are proud to share with the other two monotheistic religions. To many Diaspora Jews, the view that Jerusalem "only belongs to me" is at best childish (parents of two-year-olds will find the statement all too familiar), and at worst, against the spirit of Judaism. Israel may find that its policy on Jerusalem will alienate Diaspora Jews from the whole city, not just the Kotel.

Yes, tax laws and healthcare policy should be left to the Israeli voters to decide (although even here I would suggest that Diaspora Jews can offer us interesting ideas and new perspectives, if we would only let them). Ultimately, though, the "classic" position espoused by Avineri and others leads to a vision of Israel as a Canaanite state (I refer here to the intellectual and artistic movement of the 1940s, which saw Israel as a Hebrew-Middle Eastern state disconnected from the Jewish people and past). I don't for a moment imagine that that is what Avineri really wants. But if we want the Jewish people to be connected to Israel, then Israel has to be connected to and *considerate of* the Jewish people.

And that leads us to the third error that Avineri and others make. The position which demands that Diaspora Jews' relationship with Israel must be one of docile support and sympathy has, educationally, run its course. It may have been a powerful educational rationale for encouraging support of Israel in years gone by, but in the contemporary Jewish world, as I have argued in the previous chapters, it is no longer able to offer meaningful motivation for many Diaspora Jews, especially liberal ones, to engage with Israel. A modern understanding of 'meaningful education,' no matter which subject area, requires students to think critically and evaluate. Denying Diaspora Jew this kind of intellectual engagement with respect to their relationship with Israel cuts them off from a sense of true connection. The dialogical approach means that Diaspora Jewish involvement in Israel can and should include feeling empowered to become involved in complex conversations about all areas of Israeli society, *including its politics*.

Some forward-thinking Israelis, the most well-known of whom is probably Rabbi Dr. Donniel Hartman, have in recent years argued against the classic position espoused by Avineri and others, and have explicitly invited Diaspora Jews into Israeli political conversations. Our educational work needs to emerge much more strongly and clearly from this pro-politicization position.

Let's return, then, to Westheimer and "democratic patriotism." What might it mean to take democratic patriotism and apply it to Israel-Diaspora relations? What might "democratic Zionism" look like?

No retreat from politics

"Democratic Zionism" faces considerable obstacles if it is to get off the ground, and not the least of these is something of a double standard in Diaspora political engagement with Israel. The double standard states that you mustn't bring Israeli politics into the classroom, the pulpit, or any other Jewish educational or communal arena. These contexts must remain neutral, and politics-free, and certainly a teacher or rabbi must never express his or her political opinions out loud.

There are two huge difficulties with this position: It is impossible and it is disingenuous. Let me take each of those in turn.

It's impossible. As I noted at the beginning of this section, you simply can't engage fully with Israel without being political. Perhaps it is possible to give broad, impartial overviews of various issues in Israeli society while remaining aloof and being careful to honor the political language of all sides of a particular question. But the moment you want to actually get interesting, the moment you want to get into issues that will engage your students, you have no choice but to bring politics into the classroom. Want to study the songs of the popular rap band Hadag Nachash? Political. Want to explore the place of religion in Israeli civil society? Political. Want to learn about the successes and failures of the Ethiopian Jewish communities in Israel? Political. Anything that is worthy of study and engagement in Israel is going to be in some fashion political.

Secondly, the position that politics has no place in the Jewish educational and communal arena is utterly disingenuous. There is one set of rules for the right, and another for the left. The double standard states that it's fine for AIPAC, Stand With Us, and other "Israel advocacy" groups, to make right-wing statements that are entirely political in nature. Brief perusals of the websites of these kinds of organizations, for example, soon reveal statements that are set out as fact, but are in fact controversial and loaded political statements. The "cover" for these statements is that they are helping to promulgate official Israeli governmental policy, but even that is not always true. It's okay to be a Diaspora Jew who disagrees with Israel, as long as you out-flank it from the right (we saw this most clearly during the second Rabin administration in the mid-

1990s). God forbid you should present a left-wing political position that disagrees with Israel, though. If you do that, you're a naïve, self-hating Jew. Many (though not all) responses to Beinart mirror this line. J-Street suffers from the same double standard. One of the tasks of a renewed American liberal Zionism is to fight against that double standard.

For example, many Israel tours for North American Jews — missions, teen trips, b'nei mitzvah family tours, and so on — include elements in their itineraries that make covert political statements. Almost always, these are political statements from the right. Tours of the Golan Heights focus on the dangers to Israel's security that would be created if Syria were to regain control of the area, with no regard to the fact that many military strategists now dismiss that argument. Groups are taken to *Ir David* (The City of David), the archaeological excavations in Jerusalem, without being exposed to the problematic nature of its extremist political agenda. A popular activity is a "Bedouin experience" in which visitors are taken to commercialized Bedouin tents and offered "traditional Bedouin hospitality," without being told about the state-sanctioned discrimination suffered by these citizens of Israel.

It is claimed that these examples are not politically-tinged, since there is no explicitly right-wing political agenda in them; the experiences stand on their own, without pushing participants in a particular political direction. But this argument is false. *Absence of evidence might be — and often is — interpreted by tour participants as evidence of absence.* In other words, if you are new to Israel, and you have a wonderful experience in the archaeological excavations at *Ir David*, and that is the entirety of your exposure to that area of Jerusalem, then you are inevitably going to be more sympathetic to the right-wing Israeli narrative of "Jerusalem as Israel's eternal, undivided capital." If, on the other hand, your tour included not only a visit to *Ir David*, but also a discussion with *Ir Amim* (City of Peoples), an organization that tries to highlight the political, social and religious damage being done to East Jerusalem Arabs, then you are likely to be less sympathetic to that right-wing narrative, or are likely to view it in a more complex way. *There's no such thing as a politics-free Israel tour.* In Israel, it's all politics.

What might a democratic Zionist tour to Israel look like?

In Westheimer's essay, he includes a number of cases of how civil protest can be manifestations of democratic patriotism. For example, the mother of an American soldier killed in Iraq camped outside President George W. Bush's ranch for five weeks in order to express her anger at his administration's policies. The right to protest is a central tenet of democratic patriotism. What would it mean to take that right to protest, and put it in the hands of North American Jews visiting Israel? Some of the ideas in this section might seem radical at first read, but if we're really going to change the paradigm of Israel-Diaspora relations, we're going to have to think outside the box. And even if the following ideas are too extreme for your taste, I hope they'll at least give food for thought.

For some time now I have been imagining a "Civil Disobedience Mission to Israel." You could organize it around a variety of issues: the future of Jerusalem; state non-recognition of Conservative and Reform marriages and conversions; discrimination against non-Jewish citizens of Israel; and so on. You'd start by getting together a group of people for whom this was a really important and significant issue. For a mission like this, preparation would be crucial. You'd want people to be well-informed about the issue before they arrived, and also because you'll need to build scaffolding for participants' identities to be able to contain a "critical loyalty" to Israel. Their identities will need to be able to be deeply connected and committed to Israel but also deeply critical of some of its aspects. This isn't "Israel-bashing;" it's dialogical Zionism. You'll want to have participants spend some time reading relevant texts, talking about their Jewish identities, and doing initial research into the subject matter, before the trip itself.

It's really important to stress the preparation piece. Remember, what you're after is not just critique of Israel — there's plenty of that around. What you're interested in is a critique that goes along with commitment, a critique that sees itself as connected to Israel's ideals, principles, and future, if not its current manifestations. Democratic Zionism; dialogical Israel engagement.

So you have this group together. You've met a few times. You've read up on the issues, using Israeli news websites, books, articles, and perhaps even a carefully-chosen guest speaker or two. You've had participants think about how they can listen to Israeli conversations and take their own place within them, and about how they can develop passionate-angry-caring relationships with Israel and Israelis. Ideally, your preparations have included long-distance dialogues with groups of Israelis, with whom you are scheduled to meet as a part of your program. You've enacted a dialogical approach to Zionism and Israel engagement. The departure date is coming up. What are you actually going to do while you're in Israel?

Here are a few suggestions.

Go play with traffic

Israel's road infrastructure barely copes on the best of days: most main highways are gridlocked several times a week during rush hour. It wouldn't take much for a group of American Jewish liberal Zionists to bring the whole of Tel Aviv to a standstill. You could probably do it with just 20 or 30 people, who would move into the middle of a junction with placards and signs while the traffic lights were red, and then just remain standing there, obstructing traffic. It wouldn't be long before the media arrived, and then pictures of the placards and interviews with the protestors would be all over the news. Most Israelis aren't aware of, or don't really care about, many of the issues that are dear to liberal North American Jews; this would be a way to get them on the public agenda.

Some might argue that this kind of intrusive and frankly obnoxious public protest is counter-productive or inappropriate. I am not sure. It certainly is obnoxious; and in that, it's a controversial suggestion, but so far, alternative and more politically-correct methods have utterly, completely and abysmally failed to sway Israeli public opinion or political coalitions to take note of the concerns of Diaspora Jews. It may be a sad truth that because of the generally high level of noise in Israeli political culture, Israelis will only sit up and pay attention to issues when those issues are shouted out and made impossible to ignore. We saw this in the summer of 2011, when the social justice agenda finally became a mainstream Israeli concern. If North American Jews really want the average Israeli to think about non-orthodox conversions, for example, they'll have to be a little more direct and assertive in the way they raise the issue.

Furthermore, politically correct approaches have also been pretty counterproductive in their ability to ignite grassroots Diaspora Jewish support and excitement. In other words, politically correct approaches by definition rely on representations at the highest levels from the heads of Jewish organizations to Israeli political leaders. These discussions are done behind closed doors, are often unpublicized, and, regardless of their efficacy (or lack thereof), they have absolutely no impact on the Diaspora Jewish street or on average Diaspora Jews and the way they engage with Israel. As numerous social scientists, researchers, and pollsters, as diverse as Steven M. Cohen, Ted Sasson, Shaul Kelner, and Frank Luntz, have all pointed out, American Jews are much less inclined to engage with anything Jewishly, whether about Israel, social justice, or Bible study, if it smacks of organized, institutional, bureaucratization. They are much *more* likely to engage Jewishly if it's direct, personal, and customized. And you can't get more direct, personal and customized than sitting with a group of friends in the middle of a highway in Tel Aviv, talking to Israeli motorists about how frustrated you feel as an Israel-loving but disillusioned Jew.

Go on a camping trip

One of the standard ways in which Israeli protest groups make their voices heard is to set up tents in prominent locations. Interest groups that have chosen this path include pensioners, bus drivers, nurses, supporters of Gilad Shalit, Bedouins, Ethiopians, and, of course, most recently, the vast numbers of Israelis who camped out in support of a new social justice agenda. In many years of following Israeli politics, I cannot recall a single incident when Diaspora Jews took this course of action. Again, this relates to the point I just made about high-level representations. It's hard to imagine a senior Reform or Conservative Rabbi sitting in a tent by the Knesset. But how powerful would it be if 50 or 60 young Reform and Conservative Jews from New York, or Chicago, or St Louis, set up camp there for a week? Can you imagine the Twitter feeds, the Facebook support groups, the editorials in both the Israeli and the American press?

Again, if you find this kind of idea distasteful, undignified, or unnecessarily headline-grabbing, think back to the example that Westheimer offers of democratic patriotism in the US: the bereaved mother camping out in front of George W. Bush's Texas ranch. This kind of democratic patriotism can and should be transferable to the feelings of democratic Zionism felt by liberal Diaspora Jews.

Go for a walk

"When I marched at Selma, my feet were praying"; so said, famously, Abraham Joshua Heschel about his involvement in the civil rights movement in the 1960s. Many civil rights causes in Israel are marginalized and sidelined, for all sorts of sociological reasons, many of which are perfectly understandable and justifiable. But, whatever the reasons, the fact remains that the civil rights movement in Israel pales into insignificance compared with many of the other large pressure groups (the settlers, the ultra-Orthodox, the secular...)

One way in which American Jews might become more directly involved in Israel and more able to express democratic Zionism is by joining initiatives of the Israeli civil rights movement and in particular showing the power of simply marching hand in hand with "the other." In this way American Jews can act as literal bridges between mainstream Israelis and some of the disadvantaged members of Israeli society. I'll talk more about this below, but it's a fact that Israel is an incredibly divided society in which people live in one bubble and don't really engage with people in other bubbles. The sight of a religious but non-orthodox American Jew standing or walking in protest, wearing a kippah, one arm around a Thai worker whose child is in danger of deportation, the other arm around a Jewish secular Israeli... well, let's just say that the Jewish world has yet to see that sight, and it would be nice if we could.

What's critical about each of these three examples is that they should be done by Diaspora Jews *together with* Israelis. The idea is not that liberal American Zionists become empowered to go to Israel to argue with Israelis; it's that liberal American Zionists go to Israel to join forces with like-minded Israelis and together get involved in political issues. Ideally, Israelis and American Jews *together* should be playing with traffic, camping, and walking. That's the hallmark of complex-conversation, politically empowered dialogical Zionism.

Concerns about the politicization of Israel Engagement: Politics divides

In the United Kingdom, many politicians from different parties are friends. British politics, like those in most other countries, can occasionally become a place of animosity and deep hostility, but for the most part, it's quite... civilized. The MPs make a lot of noise shouting at each other during Prime Minister's Questions, but afterwards they mill about together in the House of Commons Tearoom. (Indeed, one elderly Tory MP recently got into trouble for affectionately patting the bottom of a female Labour MP while they were queuing for refreshments together!). The 2010 British general election was the tightest and most fiercely-contested election in a generation, but the pre-vote debates between the three party leaders were respectful and collegial. Following the election, which resulted in a hung parliament, British politicians were faced, again for the first time in a generation, with the task of negotiating a coalition; yet even this potentially divisive task was, by all accounts, accomplished quickly, respectfully, and with dignity.

In the United States, George W Bush was ridiculed by the left-wing media, and now Barack Obama is vilified by the right. Yet Republican and Democratic lawmakers treat each other, for the most part, cordially, civilly, and respectfully. The respect for the office of the President holds in check the opposition politicians' baser instincts.

In the UK and the US, politics may separate, but they don't divide. In Israel, that is not the case.

To understand Israel properly, you have to understand that it is a deeply divided country and society. Right-wing religious settlers grow up without meeting or interacting with left-wing seculars, and vice versa. Most Israelis never talk with ultra-Orthodox Jews. Israeli Jews and Israeli Arabs lead separate lives, in separate communities.

Many of Israel's divisions are not just social or religious: they are, or become, political divides too. Secular Tel Avivians vote for different political parties than do religious settlers, and each of them thinks that the other group will ultimately cause the state's destruction. Religious settlers think that Tel Avivians' hedonism and rejection of Jewish values will lead to the erosion of the Jewishness of the state, and Tel Avivians think that religious settlers' extremism and selective understanding of Jewish texts will lead the state into an abyss of eternal conflict. Neither side talks to the other, understands a view outside of their own, or can conceive of the 'other' in anything other than broad, stereotypical terms.

One reason that people fear making Israel engagement too political is that we don't want the American Jewish community to become infected with this level of animosity.

Israeli politics is about life and death

Much has been written about the political culture of Israel and why its democratic institutions are less civil than those in other Western countries. Israel is a young democracy, and many of its citizens grew up in societies without long democratic traditions. Democracy is often understood in Israel as meaning "the majority decides," and while that's of course the basic technical definition of democracy, some of the unwritten assumptions of other Western liberal democracies, like protection of the rights of democratically-defeated minorities, are much less ingrained in Israeli political and civil culture. The "tyranny of the majority" is a real occurrence in Israeli democracy, manifested in ways that would be alien and even repulsive to voters in other Western democracies.

Along with this imperfect political culture, the subject matter of much political debate in Israel is also different from that in most countries. In Israel, politics isn't about tax rates, healthcare, or environmental policy. Well, it is about those things too, of course, but the main headlines, most days, concern the ongoing conflict with the Palestinians — a topic that hits much harder than tax rates or water fees. This is about the very survival of the state. When the stakes are that high, it's extraordinarily difficult to have a cup of tea with your opponents after the debate.

So the idea of politicizing American engagement with Israel is not without its concerns. If that politicization might lead to division, distrust, and even hatred, between previously amicable elements of the American Jewish community, it has the potential to be a bad idea. Surely it's better to just remain on good terms, and avoid dealing with the difficult issues? We don't want American Jewry to fall into the deep divisions of Israeli society, after all.

This fear is real and legitimate. It may well be that the politicization of American engagement with Israel will indeed lead to greater internal divisions. But American Jewry, with its strong traditions of dialogue, communication, and respect across the denominational streams, can offer the Jewish world a powerful vision of what I call "unity without uniformity." If liberal Jewish American Zionists do begin to become more vociferous in expressing their viewpoints, then one of the American Jewish community's challenges will be how to contain this division within a broader framework of togetherness.

This will be difficult, but not impossible. One of my most memorable experiences while studying in Israel for the year as a young post-graduate in the mid 1990s was when two of my teachers at the Pardes Institute, an open, co-educational yeshivah, led a session in which they debated Israeli politics together. These two teachers were from opposite sides of the political spectrum, and were both known to be activists in the right-wing and left-wing camps respectively. During the discussion, they did not hide their differences and critiqued each other's positions quite strongly. Yet it was all done in a spirit of mutual respect and of personal affection for the opponent, and with the unwritten shared assumption that civil discourse was a paramount value in the debate. And afterwards, of course, the two of them shared a cup of tea together and remained colleagues.

This model of interaction was not typical, of course, and would be extraordinarily difficult to replicate in other contexts. Both teachers had grown up in America, with its democratic culture ingrained in them before they made aliyah; they were both colleagues in a faculty of teachers at a small, vision-driven, educational institution; and, while politically far apart, they were quite close together in terms of their religious worldviews.

Nevertheless, I believe that it is one of the tasks of American Jews, whether from the right or the left, to import the more "civilizing" elements of Western political culture into Israel. Israel seems to have succeeded in importing the worst elements of America: McDonald's burgers, rampant materialism, and an inability to win at soccer. It's about time that Israel started importing some of America's better qualities; and it's the job of American Jews to help facilitate that transfer.

Complexity applied: Postzionism

The analogy to our relationship with the Torah

We have now set out the four foundations of a dialogical approach to liberal American Zionism and Israel engagement: complexity, conversation, empowerment, and politics. My proposition is that American Jewish engagement with Israel should be a series of *conversations* about the *complexities* of Israeli society, and in those conversations they should be *empowered* to dialogue and disagree with Israelis about a variety of issues, including *political* ones.

This approach to Israel is not easy. Sometimes people feel that it challenges the very foundations of their Jewish identity and relationship with Israel. If you were brought up with the "mobilization" narrative that I discussed in chapter one, then these new ways of engaging with Israel can appear almost blasphemous. In this chapter, I want to explore that apparent blasphemy by once again using an analogy from our approach to the Torah. What I will argue here is that the approach I am advocating that we take towards Israel is extremely analogous to the approach that many liberal Jews take towards the Torah.

Liberal Judaism and Biblical Criticism

I am a liberal Jew. By "liberal," I mean, as I noted earlier in this book, that I see Judaism as a phenomenon which, rather than being purely Divine, has significant human cultural, historical and sociological influences and sources. Liberal Jews reject the fundamentalist notion that the corpus of Torah and Jewish law is literally a Divinely-authored body of work. (Some Jews who self-identify as Modern Orthodox might also agree with that statement, but in general, those opinions are much harder to voice openly in Orthodox communities).

Specifically, I tend to define myself as a Conservative Jew, but nearly all of what I have to say in this chapter relates to Reconstructionist Judaism, Reform Judaism, independent post-denominational Judaism, and also the very liberal wings of modern Orthodoxy.

I understand the core difference between liberal Jews and Orthodox or fundamentalist Jews as a disagreement about the place of historical and scientific scholarship in our understanding of Jewish history. As a committed but liberal Jew, I believe that the critical academic study of Judaism's origins and history can and should go hand in hand with commitment to Judaism in general. Orthodox-fundamentalist Jews would deny this claim, and argue that it's an all-or-nothing game: for them, commitment to Judaism in general requires abstinence from, ignoring of, or skepticism about the critical academic study of Judaism's origins and history.

This disagreement plays out most clearly in the study and teaching of Bible. At its heart, the academic field of Biblical studies, because it disputes the Mosaic origins of the Torah text, is an attack on the foundations of traditional Jewish faith. Some scholars have attempted to blur this fact, by finding precedents to Biblical criticism in medieval rabbinic commentators, or integrating source criticism within a conception of divine authorship more broadly understood. Nevertheless, the fact remains that when intentionally liberal Jews say "vezot haTorah asher sam Moshe lifnei bnei yisrael, al pi Adonai, b'yad Moshe" ("This is the Torah which Moses placed before the Israelites, through the mouth of God, by the hand of Moses," traditionally said upon raising the Torah for all to see after its having been read), they don't mean it literally. They — we — I — see the Torah as a document with, at the very least, significant human influence, bound by ancient times, circumstances, and mores, rather than the perfect, eternal, divine word. Liberal Judaism is not predicated upon seeing the Torah as the "word of God;" and therefore direct divine commandment is not the primary motivation for Jewish study or Jewish ritual.

Intentionally liberal Jews, must, therefore, almost by definition balance two seemingly opposite beliefs. On one side, they believe in the validity, legitimacy, and indeed necessity of modern scholarly research on Judaism's foundational texts, history and sociology. Whether such research casts doubt on the Mosaic origins of the Torah, or looks at the rabbinic version of the Chanukah story with a skeptical eye, or introduces the notion that halachic decision-making was deeply tied to communal sociology, that research is respected. As liberal Jews, no matter how different the conclusions of academic research may be from our collective memory or identity, no matter how spiritually challenging scholarship may be, we are obligated to study it, to honor it, to support it. Scholarship is sacrosanct; and everything that goes along with scholarship — academic integrity, intellectual honesty, the search for new knowledge, the requirement for evidence, the exposure of one's ideas and sources to one's peers for investigation and critique — is sacrosanct too.

On the other side, we also have a deep, abiding commitment to the Torah despite its non-Mosaic origins, to Chanukah despite its historical difference from the rabbinic version, and, in one way or another, to halachah despite its human sociological influences. For the committed liberal Jew, no matter where he or she may sit on the denominational spectrum, a Jewish way of life is as non-negotiable as scholarship (even if the phrase "Jewish way of life" will be interpreted differently by members of different streams). Wellhausen may be sacrosanct, but so too are Shabbat, kashrut, tefillah, and tzedakah.

Of course, this is easier said than done. It is hard to uphold these two sets of beliefs. Many members of liberal Jewish communities struggle to do so, and sometimes members of liberal communities end up leaving those communities because they find it too difficult. Leaders of all the liberal Jewish streams from time to time worry publicly about the effect of critical scholarship on their members' Jewish identities; and leaders who are too public in their discussion of academic approaches to Jewish history are often castigated. (Consider, for example, the outcry over Rabbi David Wolpe's Passover sermon in 2001, when he told his congregation that the Exodus may not have actually happened historically.) Ultimately, we need to admit that fusing Wissenschaft with commitment is, while not impossible, and while absolutely necessary, a difficult task.

Biblical scholars have been aware of this difficulty since the very beginnings of the modern academic study of the Bible. Many of the early Christian Bible scholars were criticized and ostracized by the Church and by their religious colleagues. From an equally early stage in the history of modern Bible scholarship, though, attempts were made to pre-empt these kinds of attacks. An early and fascinating example was written by the British Bible scholar Samuel Rolles Driver, late in the 19th century.

> It is not the case that critical conclusions, such as those expressed in the present volume, are in conflict either with the Christian creeds or with the articles of the Christian faith. Those conclusions affect not the fact of revelation, but only its form. They help to determine the stages through which it passed, the different phases which it assumed, and the process by which the record of it was built up. They do not touch either the authority or the inspiration of the Scriptures of the Old Testament.

This awareness of the inherent difficulties of their profession has persisted throughout the modern age of Bible scholarship. Compare Driver's statement above, for example, with this, by Israeli scholar Israel Knohl, in the postscript to his book *The Divine Symphony*:

> One of the major problems of our time is religious intolerance. A deep recognition and study of the different voices of the Bible, and of the many ideas that it inspired in the development of Judaism, may help to bring about an atmosphere of diversity and tolerance. By exposing and understanding the pluralistic character of the Bible, we can recognize that there is a place for, and significance to, the kind of debate in which the other view may also be a reflection of divine truth.

While Knohl is not explicitly "defending" Biblical criticism in the same way that Driver is, he is implicitly arguing, like Driver, that Biblical criticism can be a way of understanding God; that it can be a religious act.

Many Bible scholars do not have Driver's or Knohl's faith in the ability to bridge between their professional work and their religious life. The noted theologian Jon Levenson calls historical biblical criticism a "spiritually dangerous truth — no less true for being dangerous, but no less dangerous for being true." Indeed, it is foolish to underestimate the difficulties involved in engendering a religious identity that integrates an understanding and acceptance of the conclusions of historical-critical

Bible study with a profound spiritual and affective connection to the text of the Bible. We see this difficulty coming to life in the Bible educator and researcher Ruth Zielenziger's study of the Melton Bible project of the 1960's, in which she notes that she encountered stiff resistance when her teachers were first exposed to Biblical criticism:

> Some of the people were, understandably, hostile. They had been teach-ing for many years and were comfortable with what they were teaching. I was confusing them; I had pulled the rug from under their feet but had not as yet provided them with a substitute.

Zielenziger's "rug" is what the sociologist of religion Peter Berger calls "legitimations": the reasons why we hold to a "nomos," an orderly view of life and the world. Legitimations are the glue of minority cultures in a pluralist world, because they provide reasons for followers of the cul-ture to continue so being. Without legitimations, the nomos begins to crumble, and the culture will cease to be compelling. In a sense, Berger's legitimations are the elements of what of what the liberal theologian Neil Gillman calls the "master story" that provides meaning for the religious adherent. Biblical criticism essentially destroys much of the "master story" of traditional Judaism, and the job of liberal Jewish theologians, rabbis, and educators is to fashion, develop and promulgate new narra-tives in their place. Zielenziger's task in, as she puts it, "provid[ing] them with a substitute," is the challenge for the liberal Jewish Bible educator: to create powerful master narratives that are religiously and spiritually compelling, but within a framework that is authentic to our understand-ing of history and the Biblical text.

Any stream of liberal Judaism, then, that accepts the legitimacy of academic Bible studies and Biblical criticism, is nothing less than a pro-found attack on the logic of traditional religious faith, especially a faith such as Judaism, which is a religion rooted in history. For most of Jewish history, and for much of contemporary Orthodox Judaism, the histori-cal "truth" of Jewish collective memory serves as a powerful motivating factor for current Jewish practice and belief: you do Jewish acts because God has told you to do so. Liberal Jewish streams dispute certain key, foundational elements of the historicity of Jewish collective memory, and must therefore rely on different motivating factors for current Jew-ish practice and belief, and on more complex reasons for the retention, celebration, and continuation of Jewish collective memory. They must argue that even when historical consciousness contradicts the traditional assumptions of our religion, even when scholarly research completely undermines the myths of Judaism, our commitment to what has grown from those myths is not diminished. We do not believe that Torah is the word of God, but we study it nevertheless. We do not believe that God literally commanded us to keep Shabbat, but we keep it (perhaps in different ways) nevertheless. Because of our deep commitment to both historical consciousness and contemporary Jewish practice, we are forced to re-interpret ancient myths, to re-imagine theological positions, to re-invent legitimating formulae. But we view this as the most authentic Jewish path. Judaism is not an all-or-nothing game.

The Analogy between Biblical Criticism and Dialogical Zionism

Here's the analogy I wish to make. Just as liberal Jews seek to retain a complex and meaningful relationship with the Torah in its present form, despite their recognition that its history, origins, and present form are far less perfect than traditionally thought, so too contemporary Jews must retain complex and meaningful relationships with Israel, even as they come to accept that its history, origins and present form are also much less perfect than has been thought.

Nowhere does this challenge manifest itself more clearly than the debates around what is known as "Postzionism."

Postzionism

Postzionism is a term that may be familiar to readers, yet still rather opaque. What actually is Postzionism? Many of the difficulties in debates about Postzionism stem from the fact that scholars in the field do not agree on exactly what they mean by this term. Before I go any further, then, I need to clarify how I understand the term Postzionism and its origin.

Postzionism originally referred to a movement of young academics, primarily historians. In the late 1980s, many governmental and military archives, which had until then been classified, were opened up for public scholarly access. Now, for a scholar of history, this is like winning the lottery. Most historians must put up with going over the same old archival material that their predecessors saw, in the hopes of finding an overlooked scrap of paper that might provide them material for a new nuance or suggestion. But historians with newly-opened archives are like kids in a candy store. These "new historians," as they came to be known, found much more than scraps of paper: they found letters written by politicians, minutes of cabinet meetings, confidential memos... and, crucially, these new historical artifacts appeared to challenge many of the assumptions of their disciplines and question conclusions about Israeli history and society that had been thought to be beyond doubt.

These challenges to prevailing assumptions had more at stake, though, than the mere ruffling of a few academic feathers. What these works all had in common was that they raised issues that were contrary and even inimical to the collective memory of modern Israelis. The "religion" of Zionism held many sacred cows: that Israel had always wanted peace in the face of an intransigent Arab enemy; that the IDF, and the Haganah before it, had always acted as morally as possible; that, while Israel's early leaders may have made mistakes towards its early immigrants, they had had the best of intentions; and so on. These were truly items of faith: they were the foundations on which the modern Israeli Zionist self-identity rested. The new historians shattered those foundations.

For example, in one of the first of these works, *1949: The First Israelis*, Tom Segev painted a picture of the early years of Israel that was "far less noble and heroic than Israelis had been led to believe... Israel *does* bear part of the responsibility for the tragedy of the Palestinian refugees; it has *not* taken up every chance to make peace with its Arab neighbors; and the government *did* at times discriminate against new immigrants from Arab countries [his italics]." Other important early works in this canon of new academic scholarship included Benny Morris's *Righteous Victims: A History of the Zionist-Arab Conflict*, and Ilan Pappé's *The Making of the Arab-Israeli Conflict, 1948-1951*.

The new historiography, and later, sociology and anthropology too, challenged — and still challenges — all of these foundational assumptions of Zionism, just as early Biblical critics challenged the faith tenets on which traditional Judaism rested. For example, Avi Shlaim's re-evaluation of the build-up to the Six Day War is no less faith-shattering to a Zionist than Wellhausen is to an orthodox Jew:

> Israel's strategy of escalation on the Syrian front was probably the single most important factor in dragging the Middle East to war in June 1967, despite the conventional wisdom on the subject that singles out Syrian aggression as the principle cause of war.

For a modern Israeli or Diaspora Jew today, brought up on the belief — no, belief is not a strong enough term: on the knowledge that the Six Day War was the Israeli David's desperate, miraculous victory over the unprovoked, genocidal Arab Goliath — the mere suggestion that things may be more complex, that "of all the Arab-Israeli wars, the June 1967 war was the only one that neither side wanted," that "Nasser neither wanted nor planned to go to war with Israel. What he did was to embark on an exercise in brinkmanship that was to carry him over the brink," is no less disturbing than Biblical criticism is to the orthodox Jew. It is a challenge to foundational beliefs. And when somebody attacks your foundational myths, your basic legitimating formulae, you worry that the whole house will come crumbling down.

To sum up so far: Postzionism's roots are in academia and scholarship. It is in essence true Wissenschaft des Judentums: the scientific, academic study of Judaism without a priori assumptions about the results of that study. And just as Wissenschaft Bible scholarship is threatening to some Jews because of their concerns about what it might mean for Jewish identity, so too this kind of Israel scholarship creates, for some, concerns about Zionist identity.

Hard Postzionism and Soft Postzionism

However, the term Postzionism is also used in a wider sense: Postzionists "reject the zionist [sic] principle, inscribed in Israel's Declaration of Independence, that Israel is the state of the Jewish people, a Jewish state." Postzionism is also used, then, to signify much more than a mere academic school of thought. It is used to denote a whole zeitgeist, a political movement, a collection of thinkers, philosophers and journalists whose problem with Israel is not its history but its present and future as a "Jewish" state. "This viewpoint also gives rise to a political conclusion, according to which Israel must disengage itself from its Zionist elements, which are the foundation of its Jewish character, because they are preventing it from being a democratic state."

It seems to me critical that we distinguish more clearly between these two senses of the term Postzionism. I find it helpful to denote them as 'soft' Postzionism and 'hard' Postzionism. By the former term, I mean to signify academic historical or sociological research which calls into question many of the foundational myths of the Zionist movement. Morris, Segev, and their colleagues, are all such soft Postzionists. Soft Postzionism is in essence an approach rooted in academia, in scholarship, in the work of the new historians and sociologists. It has no a priori position on ideological political positions concerning Israel's future status. A soft Postzionist can still be a card-carrying Zionist: an acceptance of Israel's complicated and sometimes morally blurry history does not have to go hand in hand with a rejection of its present or future as a Jewish state.

On the other hand, hard Postzionists are those who do indeed call into question the validity or right to exist of Israel as a Jewish state. This distinction is an important one to stand by, because many Postzionists themselves try to blur it. In a recent collection of essays on Postzionism, Pappé writes:

> Post-Zionism is a term I used to describe a cultural view from within Israel which strongly criticized Zionist policy and conduct up to 1948, accepted many of the claims made by the Palestinians with regards to 1948 itself, and envisaged a non-Jewish state in Israel as the best solution for the country's internal and external predicaments.

The absolute and glaring lack of logic between the first and second halves of this statement is astounding but unfortunately common. The first half deals with currents in historical and historiographical scholarship; the second half with the Jewish people's right to self-determination. The sleight of hand that Pappé uses to slide between these two items must be pointed out and called into question every time it occurs.

If the adherents of Postzionism blur the lines between scholarship (what I'm terming soft Postzionism) and ideology (hard), so too do its attackers. One of the most vocal attacks on Postzionism in recent years has been the Israeli political theorist Yoram Hazony, provost of the right-of-center thinktank the Shalem Center, and author of, among other works, *The Jewish State: The Struggle for Israel's Soul*. In this book, Hazony attacks Postzionism, but focuses less on history than on past and present Israeli public figures who:

> ... are paving the way to the ruin of everything Herzl and the other leading Zionists sought to achieve. Indeed, they are pushing us toward the dismantling of Israel's character as the Jewish state.

Hazony attacks a variety of thinkers, writers, politicians and philosophers, like Gershon Scholem, Amos Oz, Chaim Weizmann, and, most of all, Martin Buber. Hazony dislikes the way that these intellectuals have supposedly created a culture in Israel that is anti-Jewish and in opposition to the idea that Israel should be a specifically Jewish state. Even the poet Yehuda Amichai is seen as suspect, someone who "cast[s] images that are deeply ambivalent concerning the Jewish political restoration." Hazony's extended diatribe is a diatribe about vision, not about history. This is precisely why it is so interesting to see Hazony blur the lines between history and vision. After a survey of some of the trends in the new history and sociology, he concludes:

> This, then, is the achievement of post-Zionism in Israeli academia. A systematic struggle is being conducted by Israeli scholars against the idea of the Jewish state, its historical narrative, institution [sic], and symbols. Of course, there are elements of truth in some of the claims being advanced

by Israeli academics against what was once the Labor Zionist consensus on these subjects. But so overwhelming is the assault that it is unclear whether any aspect of this former consensus can remain standing; and such is the state of confusion and conceptual decay among those who still feel loyal to the old ideal of the Jewish state that they themselves are often found advancing ideas that are at the heart of the post-Zionist agenda.

Again, note the slide between academic claims (some of which Hazony admits are in part true) and "the old ideal of the Jewish state."

Hazony and Pappé, then, may be on opposite sides of the spectrum when it comes to Postzionism, but they both use the same sleight of hand. Neither of them believes that you can criticize elements of Israel's origins while holding a profoundly Jewish/Zionist vision of Israel's future. For both of them, it's an either-or world. Both of them try to blur hard and soft Postzionism together.

In today's Israel, we see the either-or approach gaining ground at a frightening pace. Zionist thinkers, politicians and public figures are accused of treason and worse, merely because they express disagreement with the government's policies or an understanding of the Palestinians' narrative of the conflict. In a widely-reported controversy in early 2010 concerning grantees of the New Israel Fund, its president, Professor Naomi Chazan — a former Deputy Speaker of the Knesset, no less — was accused and attacked using all kinds of vicious epithets that do not deserve to be repeated here. Left-wing protestors have had their addresses and telephone numbers published on the internet. Israeli public discourse, which has always, of course, been vocal and rambunctious, has become much more delegitimizing of non-mainstream views, and while there are all sorts of political, sociological, demographic and religious reasons for this, what they boil down to is an inability or unwillingness in many sectors of Israeli society to distinguish between hard and soft Postzionism; between a particular approach to or conclusion about aspects of Israeli history, and contemporary Israeli politics or visions.

Postzionism and Biblical criticism

The parallels between Postzionism and Biblical criticism should by now have come into focus, but let's spell them out explicitly. Just as committed liberal Jews are able to build a Jewish identity that is sophisticated enough to encompass both the recognition of the Torah's imperfect history of development and a deep commitment to a dialogical relationship with it in its present form, so too I am advocating a relationship with Israel that is sophisticated enough to encompass both the recognition of Israel's imperfect history and a deep commitment to a dialogical relationship with it in its present form. Likewise, just as I strongly criticize Jews who believe that the only way to have a connection to the Torah is to buy into it hook, line and sinker, so too I strongly criticize Jews (whether Israeli or Diaspora) who think the same thing about Israel.

My argument can be summarized in tabular form as follows:

	Traditional	Liberal
Torah	**Orthodox Jewish:** Without a belief in the Torah's absolute and perfect Divine authority, people won't have serious and compelling relationships with it.	**Liberal Jewish:** You can have a serious and compelling relationship with Torah even if you don't believe in its Divine origin and you understand it as being a flawed text, affected by human sociology, circumstances, and imperfection.
Israel	**Black-and-white Zionist Approach:** Without a belief in Israel's absolute rightness and moral superiority in its recent history, people won't have serious and compelling relationships with it.	**New Liberal Zionist:** You can have a serious and compelling relationship with Israel even if you don't believe that it has always acted perfectly and you understand it as having a flawed history, with moments where its human actors have, for all sorts of reasons, behaved wrongly.

My own thinking about these matters has been greatly influenced by two British Conservative/Masorti rabbis, Rabbi Louis Jacobs, z"l, and Rabbi Jonathan Wittenberg. Jacobs famously split from Orthodoxy in the United Kingdom in the 1960s when he wrote a book accepting the validity of academic Biblical studies and its conclusions about the Torah's origins. Wittenberg, now leader of the UK's largest Conservative/ Masorti synagogue, offers in his first book, *The Three Pillars of Judaism*, a strident defense of the liberal Jewish position. He, like Jacobs, summarizes and accepts Biblical scholarship on the Torah. He then writes:

> To others this 'non-fundamentalist position' [i.e. the Conservative Jewish acceptance of scholarly conclusions about the Torah's origins] is abhorrent and threatening. It undermines the whole fabric of Judaism. For if we deny that every word of the Torah is literally the word of God, then we remove the absolute divine authority from Torah. Without such authority what will become of it? Who will keep it any more?

Wittenberg deflects the attack with what is to my mind one of the most insightful critiques of the Orthodox position on biblical criticism; this position, he notes, "is an argument about effectiveness, not one about truth. To the question of truth it is absolutely irrelevant." Wittenberg suggests that the orthodox attack on biblical criticism shifts the target from a dispute over historical claims to a diatribe about the possible future sociological consequences on a community that accepts or engages with those pieces of historical evidence.

So too, with regard to Israel, engagement with a particular academic school of historical scholarship is equated with the promulgation of contemporary antizionist political policies. Right-wing critics find it extraordinarily difficult to accept someone who is a soft Postzionist but opposes hard Postzionism. They can't conceive of someone who accepts the findings of the new historians about Israel's past actions, and yet remains a proud believer in Israel's existence and future potential as the Jewish people's national homeland and cultural hub.

Just as committed liberal Jews are able to develop "master stories" that provide a compelling nomos for the place of a flawed Torah in contemporary Jewish life and identity, so too our task for the Jewish world today is to enable more Jews to develop master stories that provide a compelling nomos for the place of a flawed Israel in contemporary Jewish life and identity. We need to have the courage to stand up for the critique of our foundational myths with integrity and honesty, always firm in our message, as so eloquently expressed by Wittenberg, that truth is more important than effectiveness. We need to acknowledge that this stand does mean that we have less compelling legitimations for our communities.[2] And we need to redouble our efforts to use the legitimations that we do have, the legitimations that mean so much to each of us, to expose more and more unaffiliated Jews to the nevertheless compelling power of our worldview.

In the teaching of Bible, this means uncompromising integrity about scholarly research on the Torah's origin, coupled with the unwavering belief that Bible study can be a spiritually profound and enlightening experience which every Jew should engage in, and that a Jewish lifestyle, even if human in origin, is a compelling and enriching way to live one's life. We have become quite expert at making this kind of move when it comes to Bible: witness the current debates on homosexuality, gender issues, and the like, where Bible scholarship is often brought in, but where we never hear voices that suggest that our commitment to the Torah qua Torah should be called into question.

Israel education needs to learn from this level of nuance, and help our students debate issues like Israel's actions during the War of Independence, or its maltreatment of Mizrachi communities, or its policies of settlement in the West Bank, without calling into question our commitment to Israel qua Israel. Thus in our thinking about Israel, this

---

[2] Louis Jacobs makes this admission in *We Have Reason to Believe*, when he accepts that a Conservative/Masorti Jew is less likely to adhere to the strictest rules of kashrut as a result of his beliefs about biblical criticism. Again, though, it comes down to truth versus effectiveness, and for Jacobs, the choice is simple:truth.

means an equally uncompromising approach to the findings of modern historical scholarship, to the support for academic freedom, and to the acceptance that no nation's history or present, even Israel's, is perfect.

Equally, even as we support the shattering of some of Zionism's founding myths, we must not waver from our deep-seated belief in the right of the Jewish people to have their own nation-state amongst the nation-states of the earth. As modern Jews, we are privileged, after 2,000 years in exile, to have a homeland to which we have an unquestioned right to return. We are, once again, a sovereign nation, and we have a responsibility to make that state a truly Jewish state, governed by the spirit of the prophets. Engagement with the state of Israel, its beauty, its problems, and its visions, must be at the heart of the educational enterprise for Diaspora Jews.

Yes, we need courage to stand up for these ideals. It is not easy to be a liberal Jew, and it is not easy to be this kind of Zionist either. It's much easier to say that things are all black or all white. Easier, perhaps, and certainly more effective — but not true.

Complexity isn't easy, but it's necessary

Earlier, we read how Ruth Zielenziger, training teachers in critical approaches to teaching Bible, sometimes felt as if she had pulled the rug out from under the feet of her students. As someone who trains Jewish educators to do Israel engagement, I know this feeling. The new approach to Israel engagement that I've introduced in this book is not always easy to integrate into one's Jewish identity. People can get very upset when you challenge their foundational narratives. One of my inspirations for this work is Professor Neil Gillman, emeritus professor of Jewish Theology at the Jewish Theological Seminary, who, over the course of several decades, challenged students' foundational beliefs, not about Israel, but about God.

Gillman is famous — infamous, perhaps — within the halls of JTS for making students cry. Students in his classes cry not because he is mean; he is by all accounts one of the gentlest, most caring teachers in academe. They cry because he breaks their myths, and with those myths, their hearts. Gillman's classes in Jewish theology confront students, often for the first time, with theological positions that contradict many of the "mythic" or "romantic" ideas with which they grew up. Revelation, the existence of evil, and even the very idea of God, are all explored from a diverse range of perspectives, including traditional ones, but also including radically untraditional ones. In my colleague Sarah Tauber's remarkable portrait of Gillman, she notes that, in the eyes of some of his students:

> ... he is disturbing theologically for many Conservative Jews, and that includes rabbis. His use of the word 'myth' in regard to Torah disturbs them, especially if they don't understand how he uses the term anthropologically in relation to Judaism... Some people in the movement have accused him of turning Jews away from Judaism because of his stance.

Another former student of Gillman noted:

> Most of us know about and accept the 'broken myth' idea... At the same time, and this was very powerful and unsettling for me, I think that even

though, or maybe because he understood that we live in a time when the Jewish myth is a broken one, he was also mourning that fact. Mourning it alone
and mourning it with us.

Gillman himself struggles with these questions. Gillman, writing a
self-reflective essay about his teaching over the years, is adamant about
his role as an educator:

> This crossroad between Fowler's stages 4 and 5, the focus of this entire
> inquiry, is precisely where most of my students are stuck. I understand my
> task as the attempt to get them over this hurdle, to convey to them the full
> exhilaration and liberating power of Paul Ricoeur's "second naivete."

But nevertheless Gillman admits the difficulties and challenges of
the task he sets himself. A historical approach to Judaism, he writes,
sometimes threatens to "play havoc with the religious sensibilities of students."

Gillman wants his students to stretch their Jewish identities so that
they can contain both historical-scientific-critical thinking about God,
revelation, and Jewish texts, and also deep but nuanced religious commitment. He is a true liberal Jew. Some of his students find it hard to do
this; some of them don't believe that it's possible; and Gillman himself is
painfully aware of the difficulty involved in developing this kind of religious identity. Being a committed Jew with a nuanced liberal theology is
not easy. That's why Gillman's students sometimes cry.

To return to Israel education: just as Gillman worries about the effect
that his teaching of theology might have on the religious commitments
of American rabbis, so too I sometimes worry about the impact that our
teaching of a nuanced and complex Israel, rather than a perfect-roman-
ticized one, might have on the feelings of connection or commitment
to Israel amongst my students and their communities. It's not simple to
move from a one-dimensional understanding of Israel towards a multidimensional one, so that Israel is no longer seen as a perfect and miraculous entity that must be supported and loved blindly, but as a complex,
real place, alternatively beautiful and frustrating, ground-breaking and
backward: ultimately, an unfinished product, a work in progress, an on-

going project that urges the Jewish people to become empowered to participate in its completion.

Initial reactions to being exposed to Israel's complexity often leave people feeling "off balance." Confronting points of view that challenge previously held comfortable and one-dimensional assumptions about Israel, Israelis, Israeli politics, Arabs, and religious life in Israel, can frustrate people and throw them off equilibrium. This instability is uncomfortable, to say the least, and even frightening. When people realize that the way they related to and conceptualized Israel before is no longer adequate, it creates dissonance and anger.

I've experienced these responses wherever I've taught and spoken about this new approach to Israel engagement. The dialogical approach, with the different demands it makes on the liberal American Zionist, can be controversial. It does make some people feel "off balance." It creates disequilibrium.

I would argue that such disequilibrium is probably a necessary step in the process of re-understanding Israel engagement. Disequilibrium, together with the feelings of anger, sorrow, and loss that accompany it, may not be a bad thing in the long run. A sense of vertigo can contribute to a new openness; without it, new learning may not happen. It may be extremely difficult, both professionally and personally, to see people you care about feeling off-balance. But sometimes, we need to take a deep breath and accept people's disequilibrium, defensiveness, anger, cognitive dissonance, and discomfort as they work to relax their hold on the 'safety rails' of long-held beliefs, and struggle to find new foothold in an unfamiliar terrain. We need to learn how to support our friends, congregants, and students in that phase, knowing when to listen, when to challenge, and when to push. These educational dispositions are much easier to describe in writing than to perform in practice, but stating them in writing is an indispensable step towards improving our practice. In this kind of complex and important educational and communal endeavor we cannot expect immediate gratification. Changing decades of entrenched educational and sociological cultural understandings about Israel will be a matter of evolution rather than revolution: it will go slowly.

It's not simple; but the difficulty of achieving this complicated relationship with Israel should not deflect us from its necessity.

From vision to practice

Hi-res and connected

Until now, we've explored a conceptual framework for a new vision of Israel engagement and American liberal Zionism. Vision, though, is insufficient if not translated into practice. But translating vision into educational reality is not as simple as just saying, "Well, what would this look like in practice?" One needs careful scaffolding to turn conceptual statements and ideas into educational reality. In this chapter, I'll present some of that scaffolding and begin to move from the conceptual framework into the world of practice by presenting a mapping tool that can help us analyze existing Israel educational activities — and create new ones — that are in line with this book's vision.

The ideas in this chapter are based on research that I conducted during the summer of 2006 at a Jewish summer camp in the northeastern United States.[3] During that summer, I saw many examples of Israel education, some wonderful, some questionable. My work that summer, which was further developed in collaboration with my colleagues Robbie Gringras and Esti Moskowitz-Kalman, of Makom, the Israel Engagement Network of the Jewish Agency, led to the creation of a mapping tool for Israel education, which the Makom team have since found extremely useful for analyzing Israel education and engagement. Gringras dubbed it "The Makom Matrix." It has become an important tool in Makom's educational work, as well as in my work in training students in Israel education. In this chapter, I'll describe the tool and show how powerful a device it can be to help us make the bridge between educational vision and practice.

The matrix is in essence a standard graph, with x and y axes. The x axis runs between two poles, "disconnected" and "connected," as follows:

---

[3] This research was first published in "A New Heuristic Device for the Analysis of Israel Education: Observations from a Jewish Summer Camp," Journal of Jewish Education, 2009.

DISCONNECTED ◄────────────► CONNECTED

In other words, there are some American Jews who are very deeply connected to Israel, and some who feel much less connection. Jews who feel connected to Israel feel joy at its achievements and pain at its sufferings, and Israel inserts itself into their Jewish life in many ways. Jews who feel disconnected from Israel are more dispassionate about it: they view it more objectively; their Jewish identity exists without Israel. In surveys of American Jews, one of the questions that is often asked about Israel is: "Would you view the destruction of Israel as a personal tragedy?" Jews who are disconnected from Israel will tend to answer no (and, indeed, in the 2007 study by Cohen and Kelman, more than half of Jews under the age of 35 answered that way).

But the continuum between disconnected and connected provides only a linear description of connection to Israel. Since we've established that our goal is a more complex relationship, we need a more complex way of visualizing that relationship. The addition of a second axis will help us to see things in a very graphic way.

Our complementing axis can describe the level of understanding, ranging from vague notions, which we can call 'lo-res', to involved comprehension, which we can call 'hi-res'.

LO-RES   ◄────────────►   HI-RES

Some people have only a patchy understanding of Israel's history, culture, politics, and society. On the other hand, some people have a very high level of knowledge about these issues.

The camera-pixels metaphor is helpful: at a lo-res level, people have only a vague, blurry idea about much of Israeli life, past and present; at a hi-res level, things are much clearer. A lo-res view of Israel sees the contours of a picture, the basic outlines of what is going on. As the picture gets more hi-res, one sees more and more of the details, and the picture thus gets much more nuanced and sophisticated.

These separate and very different expressions of relationship to Israel can be placed as the 'x' and 'y' axes of a graph. if we do so, it becomes possible to express both the sense of connectedness to Israel as well as the 'Israel IQ' of an individual and, in this way, to have a fuller understanding of their relationship with Israel (as opposed to merely their sense of connection to Israel)

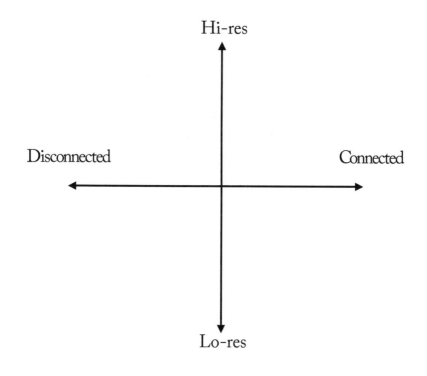

FIGURE I

The four quadrants of this graph represent four different kinds of relationship with Israel. We might suggest, with an array of full disclosures, tentative riders, caveats, and qualms about the risks of stereotyping and generalizations, that many American Jews inhabit the bottom left quadrant. As we noted, many of them, especially younger ones, relate to Israel from a somewhat "disconnected" perspective, and that engagement is often or usually done in a lo-res format: not only do they not feel connected to Israel, they don't know very much about it, either.

As we move up the y axis, it becomes clear that hi-res does not necessarily mean more "committed" or "connected." A CNN Middle East correspondent may have a very hi-res understanding of Israel, but continues to relate to Israel from a disconnected, dispassionate perspective, therefore inhabiting the top left quadrant.

In the bottom right quadrant I would suggest, again tentatively, with that same array of riders and caveats, that we find some members of the American Jewish communal leadership: those who certainly feel "connected" to Israel, who view it not as "other" or "separate," but as deeply tied to their Jewish identity, to their sense of Jewish self; such people are deeply committed to Israel in all sorts of ways, but nevertheless may sometimes retain a fairly lo-res view of what actually goes on. The complicated and sometimes frustrating complexities of Israel, which would come into sharper focus in a hi-res view, may not play a large role in their relationship with Israel.

Finally, if we look at the top-right quadrant of the graph, that's where, I suggest, we should want American Jews to be: feeling "connected," deeply committed to Israel and seeing it as an integral part of their Jewish identity, and also having a hi-res view of Israel, replete with its details, complexities, frustrations, and realities, both wondrous and worrisome. If you think about the dialogical approach to Israel engagement that we have developed so far in this book, in which American Jews are empowered to enter complex conversations about all aspects of Israeli society, including politics, I hope you'll already sense that that kind of engagement with Israel is definitely a top-right quadrant activity. Hi-res and connected: that's the goal of modern Israel engagement that this book proposes.

To summarize graphically:

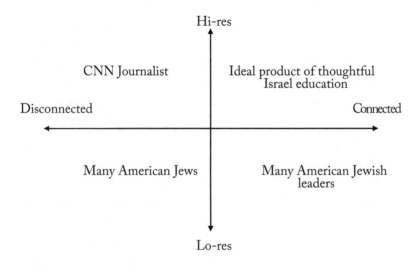

FIGURE 2

In the next section, we'll use this matrix to think about our goals in doing Israel education and engagement.

First comes love?

Let's begin by thinking about young Jews who are in the bottom left quadrant, and consider what it might mean for them to move vertically up the y-axis. Some schools of thought in Israel education focus entirely on providing students with knowledge about Israeli history and politics. The idea that drives these educators' approach is that by enhancing the students' knowledge and understanding of the country, they will foster a sense of connectedness. However, the foreign correspondent example should lead us to wonder whether things are more complicated than that. Increase in knowledge — the move from lo-res to hi-res — does not seem to directly cause greater connectedness. I'll explore this in more detail in the next chapter.

What about directly encouraging greater connectedness, or move-ment toward connectedness along the x axis of our graphical construct? For many Israel education programs, this appears to be the end goal itself. As we saw earlier in the book, some Israel advocacy organizations seek to connect young North American Jews to Israel by deliberately avoiding a hi-res grappling with difficult issues. I'll also return to this theme in the next chapter.

Even if the proponents of these kinds of programs would agree that the ultimate goal is to encourage American Jews to feel both more con-nected to *and* more educated about Israel (and I'm not sure that they would), they do all seem to start from an assumption which may or may not be correct — that Jews must love and feel connected to Israel before they can be 'told the truth' about Israel. Represented with our graphic matrix, their movement would look like this:

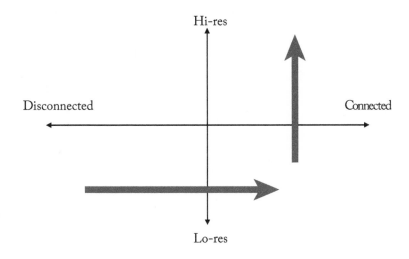

FIGURE 3

There are several problems with the "connection first, and only then, details" position. If we educators are only concerned with creating connection to Israel, while fudging or blurring the more complicated details, then we run the risk that when our students do find out those details from other sources, as they invariably will, they'll think that we've been lying to them, indoctrinating them, or treating them like children, and end up in the top left hand quadrant, retreating to a position of being less connected than they were before, even if they are now more knowledgeable. I have heard this story from countless parents of kids who went through various Jewish educational systems, only ever hearing the simplistic, mobilization narrative about Israel that I critiqued at the beginning of this book. The moment these kids get to college, and take a class in Middle Eastern Studies, or meet a thoughtful Palestinian, or read a book by Tom Segev, the bubble is burst. They feel lied to. Their connection to Israel, built on a utopian vision of idealistic wishful thinking and few actual facts, collapses.

Instead of this approach, we should create Jewish educational systems that educate for connection along with a solid understanding of Israel's flaws, foibles, and frustrations. When the Israel educator models for her students a connection to Israel that co-exists with an understanding of its complexities, when connection to Israel is built upon a more solid, hi-res examination of the multi-faceted issues, then further revelations about Israel's faults can be merged into that pre-existing identity. Hence my claim that the move into the top right quadrant can and must be done directly from bottom left to top right.

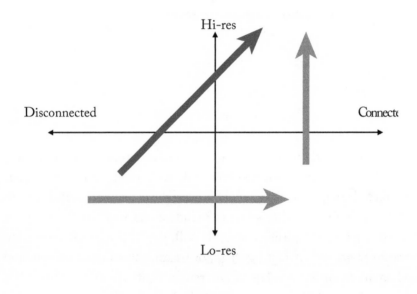

FIGURE 4

Now, it's clear that that move won't be a straight 45 degree arrow; it's more likely to be something like this:

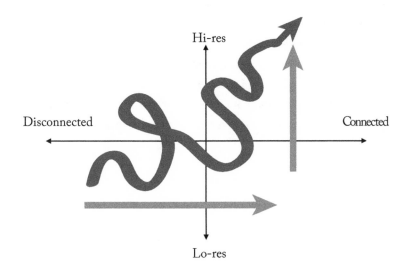

FIGURE 5

In other words, there will be some days, some moments, some activities, which move the learner in a pure horizontal direction. Perhaps a Yom Ha'atzmaut celebration would be one such event. Or perhaps party night on a Birthright trip. Likewise, there will be some days, some moments, some activities, that move the learner in a pure vertical direction: a Middle Eastern Studies course at college, for example. The thoughtful Israel educator will seek ways to move horizontal activities a little more vertical, and vertical activities a little more horizontal, and to include in the curriculum a variety of educational experiences that mix horizontal and vertical movement. In general, good Israel education will be the kind whose overall *vector* is that 45-degree movement into the top right quadrant.

Hi-res and connected Israel engagement is not necessarily dialogical Israel engagement, but it's certainly a pre-requisite for it. My sense is that the best Israel education initiatives in the American Jewish community right now are getting into the hi-res/connected quadrant, but are still not pushing into dialogical Israel engagement. The challenge in every communal and educational context, be it camp, school, synagogue, or JCC, is how to create, first, hi-res and connected Israel education activities and experiences, and then, how to leverage those into dialogical liberal Zionism, so that the involved and concerned relationship with Israel becomes a bridge towards empowered conversation about Israel.

What is 'Israel Education'?

The hi-res/connected matrix helps us think more clearly about what kinds of emphases need to be combined in order to make Israel education as effective as possible.

Israel Education is not just about knowledge

One large and vocal school of thought in the Israel education field suggests that "knowledge is power." Perhaps the primary example of this approach is the Center for Israel Education at Emory University run by my colleague Professor Kenneth Stein. The basic educational premise of this program — and it's important for me to stress that I view it as an excellent program, despite the concerns that I'm about to raise — is that a lack of historical knowledge is the main barrier to more successful Israel engagement in the American Jewish community. As the Center's website explains:

> To understand Israel today, *we must understand the context from which the state emerged.* Zionism developed in the 19th century as one of several options chosen by Jews in response to the challenges of modernity. The creation of a national territory emerged from a biblical attachment to the land of Israel, a sense of peoplehood, and prolonged denial of liberty and freedom. The road to statehood in 1948 was not easy; Zionists ultimately overcame the challenges they faced while always focusing on achieving self-determination.

We see a similar call to arms in an address some years ago by Jehuda Reinharz, then president of Brandeis University. Reinharz is even more insistent that knowledge is the problem:

> My strategic formula is the essence of simplicity: to combat the lack of knowledge, we need to create and disseminate understanding — rich in historical context, reflective of the best social scientific information we can marshal, and delivered widely and with passion.... This paradigm places the development of impeccable scholarship about the Middle East and Israel at

the forefront and ensures its utility by promoting applied research and dis-seminating it to scholars, to students, to the public and to policy makers.

Certainly there is a widespread lack of knowledge about Israel in the American Jewish community. Many American Jews have a quite limited understanding of Israeli history, culture, politics and sociology, and pro-grams like Stein's provide that information to participants in interesting and compelling fashion. But these approaches have two flaws. Firstly, they are entirely single-location approaches. They locate the problem of lack of relationship to Israel entirely within American Jewry, and assume that increasing the knowledge of American Jews will solve the issue. As I've already suggested, this focus on American Jewry as the source of the problem begins from an assumption of a one-sided relationship.

Secondly, knowledge acquisition on its own can create higher reso-lution understanding of Israel, but not necessarily stronger connection. While it's true that some philosophers of epistemology, most famously Israel Scheffler, have argued that people have "cognitive emotions" that make knowledge acquisition an emotionally satisfying activity, for the majority of people, their connection to Israel is deepened by other ele-ments in addition to simple acquisition of information. Knowledge is im-portant — critical — but it must be part of broader educational goals.

Learning happens most effectively when it is initiated by the learner's internal self-motivation to learn, not by external pressure. This state-ment has been proven comprehensively and exhaustively by educational researchers and psychologists, and is now a basic principle in the world of general education. In the Jewish educational world, however, it is often overlooked.

Isa Aron, professor of Jewish Education at Hebrew Union College — Jewish Institute of Religion in Los Angeles, gave a searing critique of Jewish education from this perspective, in a seminal paper given in 1986. Aron contrasted "instruction" and "enculturation," the first being "the act of furnishing someone with knowledge," and the second being "the process by which an individual is initiated into all aspects of a culture, including its language, values, beliefs, and behaviours."

Instruction without enculturation, argued Aron, is a "dubious enter-prise" with "little chance of ultimate success." Aron suggested that in traditional societies, enculturation happens in the home, the family, and the community, leaving the formal educational system to focus on instruction. However, in today's American Jewish community, most young Jews grow up in diverse, multicultural suburban environments, and will likely become partially enculturated into a variety of different cultures. But Jewish education systems still function under the assumption that their students are experiencing Jewish enculturation elsewhere. We are attempting instruction without enculturation, said Aron, and that is why many Jewish educational contexts fail to achieve their goals.

Aron therefore suggested a reconceiving of Jewish educational systems to include both instruction and enculturation. We can't go on pouring knowledge into learners who have no thirst for it, she argued; our job must also be to create the conditions for that thirst to emerge. Aron's approach has led to a sea-change in the Reform movement's congregational school system, spearheaded by the highly-regarded Experiment in Congregational Education project.

Our challenge in Israel education is at heart the same as in Jewish education writ large: not to provide knowledge, but to provide *motivation to seek out knowledge.*

Our problem is *not* lack of knowledge about Israel. There is plenty of knowledge about Israel out there! In fact, there is probably more information about Israel available today than most Israel-engaged Jews could possibly need, and much of that knowledge is presented in engaging and interactive style.

If American Jews *want* to find out about Israel, they can do so easily — absurdly easily, in fact. The claim that lack of knowledge is the problem has become increasingly ridiculous in the age of the internet. What is missing is not the *opportunity* to acquire knowledge; it is the *motivation* of American Jews to seek out those opportunities. In Aron's terms, our problem is not one of instruction but one of enculturation.

Aron's paper was given in 1986 and was extremely influential. So much so that, more recently, researchers Alex Pomson and Howard Deitcher have suggested that in American Day Schools, the pendulum has swung too far back in the other direction, and that *most* of what goes on in Israel education is enculturation rather than instruction. This is also problematic: Enculturation without substance is unlikely to lead to robust identity.

The approach to Israel education that I've presented in this book provides both instruction and enculturation. If I am pulled into a complex conversation about Israel, and that conversation deals with meaningful and compelling questions about which I feel empowered to express an opinion, then I will be motivated to seek knowledge that will help me become smarter about those questions. *Dialogical Israel education is an enculturating educational mode that by definition draws the learner towards the construction of content knowledge.*

Israel Education is not just about "Branding"

Another very common approach to Israel education is the 'branding' or 'advertising' approach. At the beginning of this book, I critiqued one egregious example of this approach, the *Size Doesn't Matter* campaign. Advocates of this approach agree that lack of knowledge *per se* is not the issue, and that American Jews will not seek knowledge unless certain conditions are created. However, their solution to the problem is one of marketing: Branding advocates believe that we have not "sold" Israel to American Jewish consumers in the right way, and that is why American Jews aren't engaged with Israel.

A well-known example of this approach is the study by pollster Frank Luntz entitled *Israel in the Age of Eminem*. In this study, which was based on a series of focus groups of student-age, semi-affiliated American Jews, Luntz argues that the American Jewish community uses the wrong kind of advertising to attract American Jews to Israel.

Luntz offers a list of guidelines for successful advertising about Israel, ranging from the generic (less is more; use visuals) to the Israel-specific (talk peace; don't make overtly religious appeals; relate your Israel message to America).

Many other American Jewish groups and organizations, from both the non-profit and commercial sectors, have taken similar tacks to Luntz's. A company named BlueStarPR "use[s] proven marketing know-how to create positive, persuasive posters, fliers, billboards and DVDs that build awareness and support for Israel and Jewish causes."

Many campaigns run by American Jewish organizations, often in conjunction with the Israeli Tourism Ministry, focus on training "ambassadors" for Israel who will know how to use sound-bites and other effective communication and marketing strategies to sell Israel. (This approach reached something of a zenith, or a nadir, depending on your point of view, with the infamous MAXIM magazine feature in 2007 which contained glamorous photo-shoots of scantily-clad female IDF soldiers.)

The problem with this branding approach is that it assumes that the problem is merely one of marketing, that Israel as a 'product' is similar to many other products out there, and all it needs is a decent advertising campaign to persuade a few more consumers to buy it. Again, this approach sees the problem as being entirely located within the American Jewish context.

Furthermore, as we noted earlier, this approach ignores or skates over some of the very real problems and flaws of contemporary Israel. In that sense, not only does the branding approach not increase the the numbers of those who feel connected and committed to Israel, it might even decrease it. And while a shiny advertising campaign might succeed in persuading some consumers to ignore Israel's problems, it won't work for the majority. Most young Americans today are highly sophisticated consumers of advertising, and are deeply skeptical of messages that appear to be over-managed, as Luntz admits.

Advertising Israel as a product doesn't mesh with the messages that American Jews hear about Israel from all sorts of other outlets, both Jewish and non-Jewish. It smacks of parochial bias. It makes Israel sound like a like a product being sold in a late-night infomercial.

One rabbi whom I interviewed as part of a research project for MAKOM, the Israel Engagement think tank at the Jewish Agency, bemoaned this approach to Israel education. His community was tired of it, and he was tired of it. "I don't want Israel to be just another sales call," he sighed to me. The infomercial approach to Israel education might be good pep talk material for those already committed, but it is unlikely to move the uncommitted toward engagement with Israel.

Having established that education about Israel can't be about knowledge acquisition, and can't be approached as an advertising campaign, we ought to establish what it *should* be. In order to engage the media-savvy, slightly jaded liberal American Jew, a program of 'Israel education' will need to be honest and factual while also finding points of connection and inviting participation and dialogue. It has to be high-resolution, connected, and dialogical.

Mifgash as a critical context

One of the great advances in Israel education over the past decade or so has been the increased attention paid to *"mifgashim,"* or encounters between Americans and Israelis. The notion of mifgash has been around since at least the 1980s, when it was pioneered by people such as Anne Lanski, now director of the I-Center, and Dr. Elan Ezrachi, former CEO of Masa. Mifgashim have become an increasingly important (some would say the most important) aspect of the Birthright experience: for almost half the time the American participants are in Israel, they are joined by several Israelis of the same age. Most self-respecting Israel programs nowadays incorporate significant elements of mifgash.

Encounters with Israelis are a great way to propel American Jews into the hi-res and connected quadrant. Mifgashim function to replace American Jews' stereotypes about Israel and Israelis with genuine personal encounters and friendships with real people. These relationships can serve as a springboard and 'safe space' for a whole series of complex conversations, making a 'high-resolution understanding' of the issues and the state much more likely. At the very least, when American Jews experience several conversations with different Israelis during an extended mifgash, they see that Israelis hold different opinions about most subjects. One-dimensional views of Israelis cease to be possible.

In addition, if the mifgash is structured well, with plenty of downtime and semi-structured informal educational activities, it allows space for the organic growth of connections that can lead to the kinds of understanding and engagement that will keep a participant connected to Israel long after the program is completed. Encounters can lead into hi-res, connected Israel engagement.

A fuller discussion of the techniques of mifgash is beyond the scope of this book. But we should note briefly that there is a difference between one-off encounters and extended mifgashim. A two-hour meeting between Israeli and American Jewish teenagers is better than nothing; five days on a Birthright bus together is even better than that; and several months of extended study, dialogue and interaction together is better still.

However, as we saw in Todd's response to his Israeli classmates at the beginning of this book, putting American Jews and Israelis together in a room is not necessarily a recipe for successful mifgash. Without proper intentionality in the planning, American Jews and Israelis can sometimes meet each other, feel that they have nothing in common, and revert to their pre-existing stereotypes. The course that I taught Todd and his classmates was not intended to be a mifgash; it was just an academic course that had an American mixed in with Israelis serendipitously. To make it a true, successful, dialogical mifgash, I would have had to abandon much of the academic content of the course and focus more on the relationships, assumptions, and identities of the students in the course, setting them up to be in conversation with each other.

Mifgashim, then, can be important building-blocks for the kind of liberal American Zionism that we have discussed so far, but they need to be planned thoughtfully. Unless the Israelis are prepared correctly, they can easily fall into the trap of seeing their role as the "authentic" Jew whose job it is to "save" the assimilating American Jews and "convince" them to remain supportive of Israel and Jewishly committed. On the other hand, American Jews can easily over-romanticize (or, in Todd's case, over-disdain) the Israelis they meet, and might not get involved in the hard conversations that dialogical Israel engagement demands.

Good mifgashim should give each group the opportunity to influence and be influenced. This means that we need to broaden the subject areas around which most mifgashim typically revolve.

Topics for mifgashim

In order to deepen the level or relationship we hope to foster through mifgashim, we need to broaden the subject areas around which they typically revolve. I'll address three such areas: egalitarianism, universalism and particularism, and meaning-oriented Judaism.

Egalitarianism

Israeli Judaism is much less egalitarian than American Judaism when it comes to the role and participation of women in Jewish ritual; that statement is hardly breaking news. But in most programming designed to educate and connect American Jews to Israel, the subject is carefully skirted.

Jewish ritual in Israel has traditionally been one of the most powerful aspects of a visit to Israel: the visit to the Kotel, the Friday night tisch, the Shabbat experience. For unaffiliated Jews, such experiences can be extraordinarily moving and transformative. But for moderately-affiliated Jews whose Jewish commitments include egalitarianism, increased exposure to Jewish ritual in Israel results, ironically, in increasing alienation (I am grateful to Dr. Elan Ezrachi for this point).

Until now, those who work in the field of Israel engagement, rooted as it is in the single location approach, have had no response to this problem. Our responses are usually limited to having American Jews try to just accept that Israel is a more traditional society, to set aside their egalitarian commitments, and to hope that they will nevertheless be inspired by the power of indigenous Israeli Jewish ritual. There is ample anecdotal evidence, and increasing empirical evidence, that this does not work.

Instead, the liberal Zionist Israel engagement agenda needs to turn to Israelis and Israeli society, and, in serious mifgashim, open up the complex conversation about Jewish religious egalitarianism.

This doesn't mean that Israelis need to change, and here American Jews may need to lower their expectations: Israeli Judaism, for all kinds of reasons, is not likely in the medium term to attain the level of egalitarianism found in American Judaism.

At the same time, Israelis do have to understand just how essential the principle of egalitarianism is to the current generation of young American Jewish leaders, and just how much Israelis' dismissal of Jewish egalitarianism is not just a slap in the face, but a blow to the soul.

Israeli society needs a process of political and social education that will advocate respect for women rabbis, genuine and open curiosity about egalitarian Judaism, and a willingness to seek compromises for American Jews in a variety of Jewish religious sites (the Kotel being the most visible, but far from the only, example).

The decision to engage in this process must come from both secular and religious Israelis:

Religious Israelis need to accept that while they may disagree with American Jewish choices and religious interpretations, American Jews are worthy of respectful dialogue and interaction.

Secular Israelis, for their part, need to realize that American Jewishness is not the same as the hard-line Israeli religious approach that they have come to know and hate, and that there is much in it that may be interesting and meaningful to their identities.

I am under no illusions about the enormous difficulties and barriers to these processes of political and social education in both the secular and religious communities. Nevertheless, anyone concerned with Jewish peoplehood and Israel engagement must put American Jews and Israelis in conversation together in order to raise these issues, and these conversations must focus on the responsibilities that each group has within its own community.

This is the innovation that is offered by seeing Israel engagement as a dialogical issue: tension over women's religious participation, rather than being gently side-stepped, or quietly swept under the table, instead becomes a central, compelling, and engaging basis for programming, activities, and dialogue. As well as asking American Jews to be inspired by Israeli religious passion, we must also ask Israelis to be open to learning about and to respect American Jewish commitments to egalitarianism. The goal of this kind of interactive programming would be that Americans *and* Israelis open their minds to the religious sensitivities and realities of each other. Israel engagement programs must put Americans and Israelis together and help such conversations happen.

Universalism and Particularism

Another area of disconnect between American Jews and Israeli society is universalism. Here, as before, we must be very careful with our words. The balance between universalism and particularism is a very complex navigation. Different Jewish communities over the generations have danced this dance in different ways. There are some today who would suggest that American Judaism has swung too far in a universalist direction. (This claim has been made most frequently by Daniel Gordis). Equally, there are some who would claim that Israeli Judaism has swung too far towards particularism, nationalism, and even tribalism. (Donniel Hartman being probably the most vocal in this regard).

Israel engagement that flows out of the dialogical approach will ask both groups to reflect critically, in conversation together, on their community's place on this spectrum. There's no correct answer to this question, no right and wrong; grappling with the question is an important outcome in itself.

It should be apparent how the dialogical approach might change how we approach Israel engagement in general, and mifgashim in particular, with regard to this issue.

The single-location approach usually begins by seeing the problem as an overly universalist American Jewishness, and prescribes Israel engagement as a way to swing that American Jewishness in slightly more ethnic, particularist, peoplehood-oriented directions.

The dialogical approach sees the problem as two-fold: both an overly universalist American Jewishness and an overly nationalist Israeli Jewishness.

Dialogical Israel engagement would therefore also provide opportunities for American Jews and Israelis to engage in complex conversations with each other about these questions: conversations in which Israelis may question American Jewish commitment to the Jewish collective, and in which American Jews may nudge Israelis in more universalist, outward-facing directions.

Meaning-Oriented Judaism

Mifgashim can also address another area where an American approach to Judaism tends to differ greatly from the typical Israeli approach — that of Judaism as a source of meaning in one's life. Liberal American Jews are used to seeing Judaism as a source of religious, spiritual, existential, or cultural meaning. Now, to be sure, this is a double-edged sword. For every committed Jew whose life is invested in meaning through engagement with Judaism, there is one (or more) who drifts from Jewish engagement because "I don't find it personally meaningful." Indeed, this is the great Jewish educational challenge outside the Orthodox community: Framing, mediating, and presenting Jewish engagement as an endeavor that promises meaning is the core task for every Jewish educator, rabbi, and communal leader.

Equally, the over emphasis on personal meaning is surely one of the factors behind the customized, personalized Judaism that has weakened American Jewry's ethnic ties to the Jewish people, as social scientist Steven M. Cohen often reminds us.

In Israel, Judaism is less often seen as a source of personal meaning. Most Israelis Jews who observe Jewish law do not do so because they "find it meaningful," but for a variety of other theological and sociological reasons. There has in the past decade or so been an awakening of various Jewish renewal and New Age movements amongst Israel 'secular' Jews, but, impressive and fascinating though these may be, they are still rather insignificant from a statistical perspective. Most Israeli Jews are still either *dati*, observant, or *hiloni*, secular, despite some blurring of those distinct categories in recent years. And neither of those groups sees Judaism as a source of personal meaning in quite the same way that American Jews do.

Israelis who have been exposed to American Jewry's more meaning-oriented understanding of Jewish life often come back to Israel greatly enriched by it. A common feature of nearly every Israeli organization involved in innovative and exciting Jewish educational work is that many of its leaders and founders have spent serious time in the American Jewish community.

Israelis can learn a lot from American Jews about meaning-oriented Judaism. Conversely, as I hinted above, American Jews can be enriched by such a conversation too, especially by Israelis' insistence that personal meaning can be achieved along with, and through, commitment to the Jewish collective.

Young American Jewish leaders are much more likely to feel connected to Israel and Israelis when that connection is rooted in two-way conversations, as equal partners, both sides considering how they may both change and be changed by the encounter.

Think back to Todd, Alyssa, and Rachel, and how they might be changed by this kind of Israel engagement. Todd might find Israeli voices with whom he has something in common; Alyssa might see aspects of her Jewish identity that are enriched by engagement with Israel; Rachel's relationship with Israel might become more sophisticated and worldly.

Though the three issues I have used center on one's immediate Jewish connection and experience, there are many other issues that may serve as important catalyts for complex Israel engagement conversations: the place of non-Jewish Israelis in Israeli society; the environmental challenges facing modern Israel; the return to Jewish roots in Israeli art, culture and music; the ongoing tensions between religious and secular Israeli Jews; the barriers to peace in the conflict with the Palestinians; or dozens of other issues that get at the heart of Israeli society.

The dialogical paradigm urges us to seek the complexity within issues and get people talking about it. Whatever the topics may be, though, the frame of reference for liberal Zionist Israel engagement should no longer be a single location. Israeli and American Jewish educational and communal leaders must re-imagine Israel engagement in a way that encourages American Jews and Israelis into deeper conversations together, each asking how they might enrich, and be enriched by, the other.

American Jews need to be exposed to the remarkable, inspiring experience of Israeli Jewish life as public, lived, sovereign space; to the vibrancy of Israeli ethnic-religious-cultural creativity; and to a society whose foundational civic narratives are rooted in Jewish texts and language. American Judaism is the poorer for the lack of such exposure.

But Israeli Jews also have much to learn from American Jews. Israeli Jews need to be exposed to the remarkable, inspiring experience of American Judaism as an open, pluralist way of life, which can speak to different people in different ways; to the vibrancy of the diversity of American Jewish experiences of personal spiritual meaning; and to a religious community that has succeeded in having Jewish messages inspire and infuse hundreds of thousands of non-Jews. Israeli Judaism is the poorer for the lack of such exposure.

"Influence and be influenced" must be the new catchphrase of dialogical liberal Zionist Israel engagement.

Dialogical Zionism in practice

Do try this at home

Let's assume that you have been persuaded by many of the arguments in this book so far. Let's assume that you are ready to agree that the discourse of liberal American Zionism, and of Israel education and engagement, must change in order to be aligned more authentically with the complex realities of the modern state of Israel and with the shifting dynamics of the Diaspora-Israel relationship. Let's assume that you agree that American Jews' relationship with Israel must become more multidimensional, multivocal, and complex. Let's assume that you have accepted that we can no longer teach our children to love Israel, right or wrong, but instead must try to nurture in them a passionate-angry-caring stance towards Israel, in which they are asked to enter conversations with Israelis, and effect change as well as experience inspiration. At a minimum, let's assume that, even if you're not fully convinced by all these arguments, you at least feel ready to give dialogical liberal Zionism a try. But what does that mean? How do you enact this in practice, in your family and in your community?

In this chapter, through the use of vignettes, pedagogic principles, and examples, I'll paint some pictures of what this approach can look like in practice, and how you might be able to incorporate it into your actions and interactions as an educator or as a parent.

Talking with your kids about Israel

Let's begin with the most difficult case: very young children. It's here that people often shy away from more complex approaches to relating to Israel. Surely, people say, young children should be taught to "love Israel first," and then, when they're older, they can learn about the more complex issues. I call this the 'enlightenment' approach.

The Enlightenment Approach

The enlightenment approach holds that initially one should only tell children the good things about Israel. "Let them love Israel first, and later, when they are _____ [insert arbitrary age here], we can whisper in their ears that actually, things… aren't quite the way we told you back then." There are a number of issues with this approach. Firstly, there is no agreement on what that arbitrary age is. When are kids mature enough to understand that Palestinians also might have a claim on the land of Israel? When are kids mature enough to understand that Ashkenazi Jews systematically discriminated against Sephardi Jews? When are kids mature enough to understand that Bedouin Israelis aren't treated as full and equal citizens? At what age, in other words, are children old enough to be brought through the enlightenment, as it were? To one educator or parent, the answer might be 6. To another, 12. To a third, 16. Who knows?

Another issue is a systemic one. We know all too well that children drop out of Jewish educational systems, for a whole variety of reasons: The parents move to a new town and fail to connect with the new community, or a parent loses a job and can no longer afford tuition, or the child loses interest and chooses to pursue a sport instead of complementary Jewish education. Whatever the reasons, and however much we might bemoan them, it is a fact that we cannot rely on the premise, or promise, that we can allow ourselves to tell our learners an incomplete or inaccurate version of the Israel narrative until age x, and when they're age x, we'll begin to tell them the truth. Some children will leave the school at age x-1: What happens to them?

A third, and very critical, issue with the enlightenment approach is that it can lead to a sense of betrayal, which can quickly turn to distrust and rejection. Adolescent Jews who who have been given a rose-colored picture of Israel as young children, and then learn that they had not been given the full story, may react by rejecting the entire package. "Well," they may say, "I can see that what my parents and my teachers told me about the Israeli-Palestinian conflict was whitewashed and factually questionable. So why should I accept anything that they told me about Israel?"

The enlightenment approach, comforting as it might sometimes be, is untenable in today's Jewish world. Instead, we need what I call the 'developmental' approach.

The Developmental Approach

The renowned American professor of education, Jerome Bruner, who is a specialist in the field of child psychology, famously wrote in his book *The Process of Education* (1960), that "any subject can be taught effectively in some intellectually honest form to any child at any stage of development." This aphorism has been misunderstood and distorted, but it's crucial that we understand what Bruner meant. He did *not* mean that you can teach nuclear physics to three-year-olds. Rather, you can teach the foundations of every academic discipline (including nuclear physics!) in ways that are developmentally appropriate, such that you won't have to "unteach" things later on. Bruner and his followers highlighted the problem of using inappropriate metaphors to teach children certain scientific principles; those metaphors later become barriers to further, in-depth understanding of the field.

One common example of this misuse of metaphors comes in teaching about photosynthesis, the process whereby plants convert carbon dioxide into sugars. Sometimes, young children, when they are first taught this subject, are told that the plants "eat" the carbon dioxide and "discard" oxygen. This metaphor uses what children already know about the way that human beings work and asks them to transfer that knowledge to plants. However, scientists argue that this inhibits deeper understanding of photosynthesis later on. The metaphor "takes hold" and prevents students from really understanding what is going on, which is sufficiently different from human digestion that the metaphor not only does not serve its purpose, but militates against its purpose.

In Israel education, too, we must be careful not to teach young children things we will have to "unteach" later on. The developmental approach emerges from Bruner's position: that from day one, children can handle complex subject matters when they are taught in supportive, developmentally appropriate ways.

I am not suggesting that we tell four-year-olds that Israeli soldiers killed Palestinian civilians in the 1948 raid on Deir Yassin. This is how the developmental approach can be caricatured, and it is an incorrect caricature. The developmental approach would instead have teachers think very carefully about the kind of *language* they use in talking about the conflict with the Palestinians. At age 4, it is inappropriate to even mention the conflict, unless the child asks about it. But the following "conversation stems" may give an idea of how thoughtful teachers and parents can talk about the Palestinian-Israeli conflict to children of different ages:

At age 4:
"We are very excited that many of our friends from the synagogue are going to visit Israel this summer. How wonderful! Israel is a very special place, and we hope to visit next year. Israel is a special place to all kinds of people, not just Jews: Christians, Muslims, Arabs — all kinds of people from different religions and different countries think that Israel is really, really special. Sometimes those different people have arguments with each other because they find it difficult to share Israel with each other — kind of like how you sometimes have arguments with your friends about your toys."

At age 8:
"How cool is it that your friends, Josh and Jason, are going to visit Israel this summer? Hopefully we'll go next year. Israel is basically a really safe place to visit, not like you see on the news. We honestly hope there

will be peace, and we know that most Israelis and Palestinians do too, even though there are some Palestinians who don't want to make peace with us, and to be honest there are some Israelis who are not helping make peace either. It's a little more complicated than that, and as you get older, we'll talk more about why it's so complicated. Anyway, let's make sure to invite Josh and Jason over when they get back, and we can hear about their trip from them. Is there anything you want to ask about now?"

At age 12:

"Take a look at cousin Daniel's Facebook page with his Israel photos posted on it. What a beautiful place Israel looks to be. I'm so excited for our trip this summer. You know, the Israelis have done some amazing and wonderful things, but they've also done some things that I believe were wrong. Sometimes I get pretty frustrated about some of the stuff that goes on there. When we're there, we're going to meet all sorts of inspiring Israelis, and learn about many different Israeli opinions, and we're also going to meet some Palestinians while we're there, to try to learn more about their feelings, hopes and dreams. We're Jews, and we have a responsibility to Israel, so we need to learn about what's going on, but we also need to have the confidence to disagree with Israelis when we think they could be doing things differently." (Note here the groundwork-laying for the dialogical approach).

By age 16, young people are mature enough to handle most of the elements of the Palestinian-Israeli conflict, and, even if they're not, it's impossible to hide those elements from them any longer, given their independence and the total availability of knowledge on the internet. A 16 year-old who has been brought up in a "bubble" where Israel has only been presented in a romantic-idealized light runs the risk, as I've suggested, of feeling betrayed when she discovers things that had been whitewashed in her earlier educational moments. But the 16 year-old whose teachers and parents have honestly responded to their questions in an age-appropriate and forthright way will not be taken by surprise when they encounter negative portrayals of Israel or Israelis in the press or on the web, because they will already have been exposed to this information in a way that they can handle. That 16 year-old will be more likely to continue to have a relationship with Israel, even if they feel upset at times over situations they learn about.

Let's take another example and see how it might play out with younger kids: gender issues in Israel. Clearly, I'm not suggesting that we tell four-year-olds about sex slaves in Tel Aviv; again, that's the caricature of this approach. But let's work backwards, starting with high school students. A complex, nuanced, holistic, dialogical approach to Israel engagement and liberal Zionism means opening up the good and bad about Israel and having the relationship be rooted in wonder and enrichment and joy at the good, together with a realization of, grappling with, and desire to ameliorate, the bad. So a high school unit on "gender and sexuality issues in Israel," could include activities looking at, for example, the sexual freedom of Tel Aviv versus the ultra-Orthodox pressure against that from Jerusalem; secular beach life on Shabbat in Tel Aviv; demographic issues in different communities (secular birth rates versus Arab and ultra-Orthodox ones); modern Israeli love songs; Walk on Water, a recent Israeli movie dealing with some of these issues; sex slavery in parts of Tel Aviv; achievements by women scientists and politicians; the inequalities in pay and conditions that still exist; the problems of American women rabbis in Israel; etc etc. If Israel's difficulties and flaws are taught in the broader context of a curriculum looking at a wide variety of issues, then they'll be digested, understood, and internalized by children within an environment of support for Israel qua Israel. Then, there is no danger of their later feeling the sense of betrayal that the enlightenment approach can sometimes lead to.

Middle school kids can begin to tackle some of the above issues in developmentally appropriate ways. For example, when they begin to learn about the American constitution and political system in their social studies classes, their teachers in Jewish educational contexts can teach about Golda Meir on the one hand, and ask the students to consider why Israel has such a low percentage of female Knesset members on the other. (Although, for the record, the numbers aren't that much worse than in the

U.S.: Women currently make up 20% of the Senate, 19% of the House of Representatives, and 18% of the Knesset!)

This kind of approach for middle school kids mirrors much of what we know about good educational technique in the world of general education. A good social studies teacher, for example, who wants her students to engage with a complex issue — capital punishment, say — will ask her students to research the various sides to the argument, come to class, and be prepared to have a thoughtful debate about the issue. We know that one successful way to get students to feel engaged in an issue is to encourage them to take a stand on it. We need to learn how to do this in Israel education too.

An overtly sexual curriculum may be deemed inappropriate for younger children. But let's consider some sentence stems that can serve as building blocks for these highly complex issues later on:

At age 8:
"Isn't it exciting that our Rabbi Paula is leading a trip to Israel this summer? She's so great. You know, it's pretty hard for her to go to Israel, because in Israel, most people don't really accept that women can be rabbis. So Rabbi Paula goes to Israel because she really cares for it, but it's not easy for her being there. That's kind of complicated, isn't it?"

At age 4:
"You know how we have 2 kids in our family? Well, in Israel, some religious families have 8 or 9 kids in their family! Wow — what do you think would be some of the good things about having that many brothers and sisters? And what do you think would be some of the difficult things?"

This is an educational approach that requires anticipation, forethought and preparation. One needs to be familiar, not only with the issue, but also with the intellectual abilities of the student/child. While it helps to have age-appropriate phrases and concepts in mind, it is also quite important to listen carefully to what is being asked and respond to that. An evasive answer or a "canned" answer will not inspire the trust that is needed to grow the kind of complex love we seek to plant. Especially with the conversation stems for younger kids, teachers and parents need to do a lot of preparation work before using them. These are not phrases that can be pulled out of your sleeve at a moment's notice. You need to think about the complexities of the subject at an adult level; work backwards, thinking about how different age kids can slowly engage with the fuller complexities as they get more mature; and then consider how your child, at her age and developmental level, could engage with one aspect of the issue, without whitewashing or telling her things that you'll have to unteach later, but in a way that hints at complexity in a supportive and developmentally-appropriate manner.

But the truth is, we do this in every other aspect of our parenting. Forget about Jewish issues: when it comes to crime in our neighborhood, family break-ups in our community, global warming, security at the airport, or any other complicated issue, we spend a lot of time as parents and teachers thinking carefully about how to talk with our young children about these issues, and we develop sophisticated conversation stems for them. With Israel, we need to do the same.

Talking with your friends about Israel

People in their 50s and above tend to be more conflicted about, or downright opposed to, the approach discussed in this book, than younger people. Those who remember the events leading to the birth of the modern-day State of Israel, or those who lived through the fraught period prior to the Six-Day War, when it seemed that Israel was about to be annihilated, are often wary of saying anything that has the whiff of criticism. If we look back at the 'mobilization' narrative discussed at the beginning of this book, this is the generation who came of age at that narrative's peak.

Of course, it's not just people of those generations who are strongly attached to the mobilization narrative; many younger American Jews, for a wide variety of reasons, also find it compelling and will tend to become confrontational when they hear statements that threaten the narrative of 'Israel as underdog.' How do you engage people like this in productive conversation?

Kosher Israelis

One tactic is to generate a large repertoire of articles, quotes, op-eds, or YouTube videos about what I would call "Kosher Israelis": Jewish, Zionist, mainstream politicians or public figures who have gone on record criticizing Israeli policies. It is much harder to cling to the "Zionism as Israel Advocacy" approach, in which media critique of Israel is automatically suspected of being biased, when that media critique is done by mainstream Israelis. Reading the Israeli press on-line for just a few weeks will yield an array of valid opinions that are both supportive of, and at the same time critical of, the state of Israel.

Share these articles with friends and family via Facebook, email, or print. One of the major challenges that the dialogical Zionist approach faces is that it must push back against a loud public Jewish discourse that is still rooted in the mobilization approach, and a mindset that Israel is right even when it is wrong. Because this attitude is still quite dominant, it is consequently "louder." Using various forms of social media communication might be one tool to even the balance a bit, allowing dissenting voices to be heard in a respectful and informative way.

Metaphors for Dialogical Zionism

Another very useful technique in opening people's minds to different ways of thinking about Israel engagement is to develop a list of metaphors that explain the approach. For example, my colleague Roberta Bell-Kligler likes to talk of Israel-Diaspora relations as a ballroom dance, where each partner needs to be attentive to the other's moves but sometimes do very different things. Another colleague, Steve Israel, likes to talk of Israel as a grand drama, Diaspora Jews being an involved audience.

One of my preferred metaphors is that of following a sports team. If you observe the online debates, talkbacks, and blog posts of supporters of any major sports team, anywhere in the world, you'll quickly notice some fascinating things. Supporters are very passionate about their team; but that passion doesn't always translate into docile support of everything their team is doing. Indeed, the *most* passionate supporters are often the ones who are the *most* critical. "Why did the manager buy that player? He's rubbish — he should have bought that other player instead!" "Why did the coach use that tactic? I knew it would never work!" "This player is past his prime and we need to sell him now while we can still make a profit on him — why on earth don't the club see that?" And so on. Sports fans support their team like I want dialogical Zionists to support Israel: with passion, but feeling that they have so much of a stake that they are willing to complain, to express their anger, and to suggest different ways of doing things.

Let's continue the metaphor and think about things from the team's perspective. The players are the ones who are actually doing the work. They're on the field, week in, week out. The supporters aren't, and, truth be told, the supporters don't know what it's like to be a player. But you never hear the club telling its supporters to shut up, to stop expressing their opinions, to close down the web forums with these vibrant discussions.

The sports metaphor is suggestive of "loving an adolescent," of dialogical Zionism, of much that I have spoken about in this book. The phenomenon of passionate-angry-caring sports fans is very familiar to us all — and so it's a very helpful metaphor in opening people's minds to different kinds of Israel engagement.

There is another metaphor that I like to use when people critique this approach by saying the following: American Jews don't live in Israel, don't pay taxes there, don't serve in the army... so why on earth should they have any say about what goes on there? I critiqued this position earlier in the book from a conceptual perspective, but here's a nice metaphor that you can use if you're having a discussion about Dialogical Zionism and your conversation partner plays the "you don't live in Israel" card. The metaphor is that of a therapist or good friend. When you're having a problem, or struggling with a personal issue that you can't make headway on, sometimes you go and talk it over with a friend, or, if the issue is one on which you feel you need more professional help, with a therapist. That friend or therapist will offer you advice and sometimes, perhaps, suggest actions, behaviors, or ideas that you hadn't previously thought of, or suggest that you make certain changes in the way you currently approach the issue. Could you imagine saying to that friend or therapist, with unbridled indignation: "Now hold on a minute! You're not me! You don't live in my shoes. You don't know what it's like to live in my house, you don't have to deal with my boss, you're not in my head. Who the hell are you to give me advice?"

Of course we would not dream of doing that. We understand that even when someone is not literally standing in our shoes, they can offer us advice. In fact, their different perspective — the fact that they might see things that we can't see from where we stand — is often precisely what we seek from them. We know that ultimately, the decision will be ours, and that we'll be responsible for our actions after listening to their advice; but we are also sensible enough to weigh their advice and perspective before we act. Of course, there are certain demands that we make on a friend or therapist before we'll trust them with our concerns, demands that will probably sound very similar to Nel Noddings's definition of "caring" that we explored earlier in the book. But once we're satisfied that our friend or therapist does care about us, and is listening to us, we are delighted to listen to their outside perspective on our own issues.

The analogy to Israel-Diaspora relations should be clear. The "you don't live here" argument doesn't hold water. Israelis can and should be open to advice from Diaspora Jews if the latter are doing so from a caring position. It doesn't matter that Diaspora Jews aren't drinking the water here; their perspective can still be useful.

When I've used the sports and the friend/therapist metaphor in conversations about Israel engagement, I've found that they simply and naturally "ring true" with my interlocutor, and open the door to thinking a little more out of the box about Dialogical Zionism. I offer them to you here, and invite you to make use of them too.

A Picture Can be Worth 1,000 Words

A great resource for sparking complex conversations about Israel are the pictures of the Israeli photo-journalist Alex Levac. Levac's photos have appeared in the Israeli press over the past four decades, and since 1993, primarily in Haaretz. They are candid shots, sometimes quirky, sometimes amusing, sometimes horrifying, and always intriguing, opening windows into the contradictions and complexities of Israeli society. Some of the most successful shots have been published in three book collections.

To give you a taste of Levac's style, and how his photos can generate powerful conversations about Israel, here are three, together with my annotations about how I would use them.

This first picture raises the question: What does a Jew look like? Or even, what is a black Jew? The ultra-Orthodox Jews are typical images of the religious Jew, and what a lot of people, both Jews and non-Jews, think of when asked to picture a religious Jew. Yet the dark-skinned Jew in the middle of the photo can be a catalyst for different questions. Is he what we imagine when we try to picture what a Jew looks like? My guess is that for most Americans and American Jews, the answer is no. What does that say about us? What does that say about the American Jewish community? We all know that Jews are diverse, from all kinds of ethnic and racial origins, but how diverse are our communities in real life, whether in Israel or America? Questions about Israeli society can also be asked: What is the relationship between the picture's black Jew and the ultra-Orthodox Jews around him? What do they know of each other? In what way do they see themselves as part of the same civic entity?

Finally, what do we feel with regard to the ultra-Orthodox Jews in this picture? Do we see ourselves as connected to them? Do we really share anything with them on more than the nominal level?

© Alex Levac

The second picture, taken in one of Northern Israel's National Parks, highlights another set of powerful conversations and complexities of contemporary Israel. You have the tension between religious and secular, and between Arab and Jew. Israel can't be understood without reference to both of these relationships. Presumably, for most American Jews, the women in the foreground appear "normal," and the Arab woman in the background "exotic." How do we manage our relationship with the exotic in Israel? What do we make of this traditional woman refusing to sit at home, but to go to a National Park, and sit in the waterfall in full clothing? What tensions and internal dialogues might be present in her decision? And look more closely at the women in the foreground — both are blonde. Now, it could be that they're tourists, but let's assume that they're Israeli. If they're blonde, they're not "indigenous" to the area in recent generations. And yet they feel native; they're celebrating a day out at their National Park. What is their relationship with the Arab woman? There are so many layers — newcomer vs. old-timer, religious vs. secular, Arab vs. Jew, modesty vs. sexuality… which of those conversations would you want to jump into from this picture?

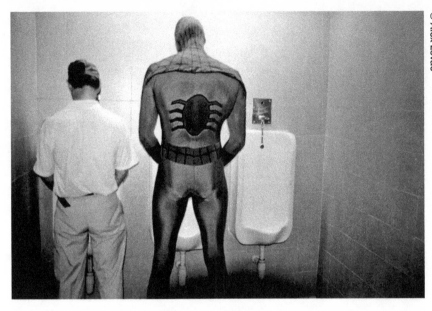

The third picture is unlike the first two: It could have been taken anywhere in the world — anywhere they have costume parties, at least. There is nothing quintessentially Israeli about it. If you were shown the picture cold, you would have no idea where it came from. But that's another important piece of the Israeli conversation: Much of what goes on in Israel is indistinguishable from anywhere else in the world. Especially in these days of increasing globalization, Israelis are eating the same pizzas and burgers as not only Americans, but Chinese, Russians, and Europeans too. Israelis go to cafes, watch movies, listen to music, and watch Big Brother on television. Is that a good or a bad thing? Does it come as a relief that Israel is in many ways the same as us, or does that in some way take away its magic? Arnold Eisen and Michael Rosenak, in an essay published in 1997 but still influential today, put it in the following way: "To the degree that Israeli culture is authentically Israeli, growing out of the Israeli reality and responding to its particular circumstances, it will be inaccessible to most American Jews. To the degree that it partakes of the universal modern culture of the west, it will be accessible — but not especially Israeli, and so not a worthy part of an Israel experience." How does Spiderman at the urinal get us into that conversation?

Give money to Israel... differently

A change in our approach to Zionism and Israel engagement does not mean that everything we have ever done with respect to Israel must be upended. Just as we look for a more nuanced and complex approach to knowing and relating to Israel, so we seek more nuanced and complex ways to continue to support Israel, even if we don't agree with everything about it.

As one example, Zionist philanthropy used to be based on a paradigm of donating to an umbrella organization, and letting the organization determine where the money should be directed. If we have learned that there are specific issues in Israel about which we feel passionately, then it follows that we need to donate the money directly where we feel it will help the most. Even with respect to causes that are not necessarily Zionist, for example cancer research or animal welfare, we can donate to Israeli causes, supporting our beliefs as well as a country we love and believe in. Giving tzedakah can be a powerful and moving physical manifestation of an ideological or religious commitment. However, one way in which a new dialogical Liberal Zionism might differ from old ways of Israel engagement is the *way* in which we give money to Israel.

The old mobilization narrative asked people to give money to Israel in the same way that it saw Israel: monolithically. You give a bulk sum to your local Federation, and they decide what to do with it. A natural outgrowth of education about the complexities of Israeli society would be an increased sensitivity to where one's donations ought to be directed. Conversely, in order to properly direct one's donations, one would need to be well-educated, and to have given the issues some thought. We should be encouraging American Jews to research smaller organizations with narrower foci, organizations that they genuinely feel an attachment to, and to give money to them more personally and more directly. Rather than give $1000 to the Federation, and assuming they'll give, say, half of that to Israel, I should be doing the investigative legwork and the thoughtful evaluation about which Israeli charities I want to give $500 to. If I'm a liberal leaning Jew, I should be giving that money to the New Israel

Fund, or Americans for Peace Now, or the Association for Civil Rights in Israel. If I'm a Conservative or Reform Jew, I should be giving money to the Israeli Masorti or Reform movement, who do so much work to push the envelope of pluralist Judaism in the most difficult societal circumstances. And let's take it a step further: if I'm an animal-lover, I should give money to an Israeli dog shelter. If a family member of mine has died from cancer, I should give money to the Israeli Cancer Research Fund. And so on.

There are plenty of ways in which you can make this change in your own life. Many of us, as we approach significant birthdays past a certain age, decide to celebrate them modestly with friends, often adding a sentence to the invitation asking guests not to bring gifts. Instead of that, why not consider adding the following text instead:

> *Please do not bring a gift; your presence will be enough.*
> *However, I would be thrilled if you would consider a small*
> *donation to one of the following Israeli charities:*
> *[here enter a list of 4-5 diverse Israeli charities]*
> *I would be even more thrilled if you would write me a sentence*
> *or two on a piece of card about why you chose that specific charity,*
> *and bring it to my party for me to collect and collate.*

No doubt you'd be able to come up with something that "sounds right" for you and your friends; but I hope you get the idea.

Talking about Israel on campus

One of the hardest places to enact a Liberal Zionist approach is on the university campus, where Israel is not just criticized, but delegitimized. Many critics of Israel also live in a world of black and white, unable to see gray: For them, Israel's faults deny it its right to exist at all. While other countries make mistakes, sometimes terrible ones, and are criticized, sometimes harshly, Israel is the only country whose right to statehood is called into question for actions that would pass without notice if done by any other country.

There is no doubt in my mind that the delegitimization of Israel is real, is rooted in anti-Semitism, and should be condemned. There are organizations like CAMERA, Honest Reporting, the ADL, and others, who do an honorable job of pointing out the inconsistencies and hypocrisies of Israel-haters to anyone who is listening. It's a thankless, necessary job, and I'm glad that I don't have to do it.

In hostile environments such as a campus, however, it is quite tempting to 'buy into' the either-or mindset, and to pretend that Israel is flawless. If we express our qualms about certain policies, if we "wash our dirty laundry in public," won't it just give further ammunition to the anti-Semites and anti-Zionists? I speak from painful personal experience. Some of my op-eds that have appeared on the Haaretz website have been cut and pasted out of context onto sites run by Israel-haters. Israeli politicians encounter this phenomenon on a much larger scale. Some years ago, for example, Ehud Barak expressed concern that Israeli was "in danger of becoming an apartheid state"; within minutes, these remarks were no longer confined to a Jewish-Zionist-internal constituency, but part of the public domain of the internet at large. In today's internet world, there is no point in debating about whether we can raise complex or difficult questions "just to insiders" while keeping a "party line" to the outside world.

So maybe we should just bite our tongues?

But this kind of a reaction allows politics to trump education, and that is not healthy for anyone. Education is about understanding the complexities, nuances and depth of the subject matter; politics is about pragmatic results in a dirty world.

I certainly understand those who would mute complexity at a time like this. But we do ourselves a disservice, and ultimately we do Israel a disservice, if we allow external criticism to dull our right — our obligation — to be critical *and* loyal; to be thoughtful, dialogical lovers of Israel. If our relationship with Israel only functions on the political advocacy level, then ultimately it will wither, and that in turn will damage our communal ability to defend Israel when it truly needs defending. We need to find ways to have political advocacy and education co-exist.

The challenge for liberal Zionists is how to defend Israel from vicious and unfair attacks while at the same time retaining the ability to be critical and troubled by aspects of Israel society and policy that we consider to be wrong.

One major challenge for the critical Zionist on campus is how to distill this critical-but-committed position into the concise, sound-bite-friendly statements that are needed, whether in campus discussions, interviews with local media, or conversations with friends.

It can be done. Look, for example, at the following statement:

> I agree with you. The current government of Israel has some deeply mistaken policies. Its policy over the occupation [or Sudanese refugees, environmental issues, Orthodox hegemony, not appropriately punishing soldiers who act brutally toward Palestinians] makes me furious. But you have to understand that there are lots of Israelis who also feel that way. There are some really impressive Israeli leaders who make me proud to be a Zionist and proud to be a Jew. I think *you* would also find their positions compelling. Let's talk about the different policies of Israel's opposition parties and how we can strengthen them from abroad.

Or this one:

> I also think Israel should leave the territories and enable the establishment of a Palestinian state; so do thousands (probably millions) of Israelis. There are some fantastic Israeli non-profit groups that are doing that advocacy work. Let's talk about how to work with and support those Israelis to make it happen.

These statements constitute a model for how liberal Zionists on campus can retain their integrity with regard to their legitimate criticisms and their responsibility to defend Israel. They are built on a three-step foundation:

1. Agree.
2. Mention the diversity of opinion within Israel
3. Encourage a deeper look.

Each statement begins with a candid and frank acknowledgement of Israel's imperfection. In confrontational situations, this is a bold step, but it has the advantage of wrong-footing the Israel-hater. Next is a statement that destabilizes the monolithic picture of Israel that many non-Jews (and Jews) have. Israel contains a wide variety of voices and opinions, and while I disagree with some, there are other, deeply compelling voices with which I strongly agree (compare my discussion of Zakovitch earlier on). Thirdly, the statement ends with another wrong-footing maneuver: a call to cooperate in the spirit of the two-state solution that guarantees statehood for the Palestinians and security for Israel as a Jewish state, based on international documents like the Roadmap, Annapolis and the Geneva Accords. Implicit is the demand for recognition of Israel's right to exist, which in confrontational situations must be a basic and first requirement for continued debate.

This last point is to be stressed. We need to distinguish between three kinds of criticism against Israel. Firstly, liberal Zionist critique of particular policies or positions that is responsible and reasonable, whether it comes from Israelis, diaspora Jews or non-Jews, should be defended as absolutely legitimate (this point should by now be obvious from the thesis of this book).

Secondly, and on the other extreme, is anti-Zionist critique that does not accept Israel's right to exist. This is clearly unacceptable and those who make it should be called out on it. As even Norman Finkelstein recently argued, if you criticize Israel without explicitly supporting its right to exist alongside a Palestinian state, you have no legitimacy yourself.

The third is somewhere in the middle, and requires more careful dissection. This is the kind of criticism that comes from people who do not seek Israel's destruction. They accept its right to exist and therefore are Zionists whether or not they accept that designation. Nevertheless, either consciously or subconsciously, they criticize Israel more than other countries, or hold Israel to standards to which they would not hold other countries.

Some Israel advocates attack this double standard, but a better tactic is to embrace it. While it's true that the Syrian government engages in wanton murder of its own citizens, the Chinese government practices draconian censorship laws, and most Middle Eastern societies are virulently anti-homosexual, none of these issues gets the press coverage Israel does. So yes, we should point that out. But we should also say that we're *happy* that Israel is held to a higher standard. We do believe that Israel, as the inheritor of the biblical Jewish tradition, has more to live up to than other countries, just as we as Jews set ourselves higher moral standards. In this way, the Jewish Zionist can dialogue with the "unwilling Zionist" about a joint vision of Israel, continually pointing out the double standard, while bringing the unwilling Zionist into a profoundly Zionist conversation about what Israel might aspire to.

This three-step approach that starts with agreeing that Israel is imperfect reveals whether your interlocutor is an out-and-out anti-Zionist or just an outspoken critic of Israel (what I'm calling here an "unwilling Zionist"). The out-and-out anti-Zionist will dismiss your calls for co-operation with the Israeli left and will refuse to accept the non-monolithic nature of Israeli society. In front of an audience, this can give you the moral high ground very powerfully. If your interlocutor is merely an unwilling Zionist, though, the three-step approach has the potential to turn him into an ally of the liberal Zionist movement. His genuine and authentic criticisms of Israel will not go away, but you have opened the door to his learning about Jewish, Zionist people and organizations which share his criticisms and yet are deeply committed to Israel *qua* Israel.

To paraphrase Woody Allen, just because they're anti-Semitic, doesn't mean to say that they're always wrong. In other words, just because a criticizer of Israeli governmental policy is anti-Semitic, it doesn't mean that discrete elements of that criticism are wrong. Liberal Jews need the courage — and that is the right word — to be able to say that out loud, to be able to sift out of the disgusting calls for Israel's destruction the real and legitimate concerns about some of its current policies.

Ultimately, an approach like this will lead to a healthier and more robust relationship between American liberal Zionists and Israel, and more effective Israel advocacy. As I noted earlier in this book, Israel advocacy is not the same as Israel education.

As represented graphically above, Israel advocacy is one aspect of the larger domain of Israel education, but not all education about Israel is 'Israel advocacy.' In fact, not all Israel education designed to serve the cause of Israel advocacy actually succeeds. Someone who has been educated about Israel in a rich, dialogical, passionate-angry-caring fashion, will be a much better Israel advocate on campus. Someone whose connection to Israel is built on flimsy sound-bites, questionable facts and sexy images will ultimately fail as an advocate.

On campus, the challenge, then, is two-fold. On the one hand, we do need to stand up to those who would deny Israel's right to exist. We can show them that we can be critical of Israel and still love it, that we can voice our frustration, our anger, and even our disgust with some of its policies, while supporting with unshakeable conviction its right to exist and flourish in peace. We also need to educate fellow Jews who are stuck in the "zero sum game" Israel advocacy mode that you can be a loving Zionist and still criticize Israel, sometimes vociferously.

And we can do all that with sound bites, too: "Israel. It's flawed. I love it. Help me improve it."

Dialogical Zionism despite the "Double Standard"

I've mentioned the double standard of international diplomacy, in which Israel is often singled out for its misdemeanors while other countries and their felonies are ignored. I suggested that instead of being angered by this double standard, we should embrace it, as authentic followers of the Biblical prophetic tradition. I want to spend a little time expanding on this through the lens of the Book of Amos.

In the first chapter of the book, Amos rails against the nations surrounding Israel, listing their sins and resulting punishments that God will mete out. None of Israel's neighbors are spared this wrath: Damascus, Gaza, Tyre, Edom, Ammon, and Moab; even Judah, the Southern Kingdom. (During this period, there was no united "Israel" as during the reigns of David and Solomon, but two separate kingdoms, one in the South, "Judah," and one in the North, confusingly also referred to as Israel. Amos, although originally Judean, prophesied in the Northern Kingdom of Israel, and there was no love lost between the two formerly united but now bitterly divided kingdoms.)

By the time Amos has finished with Judah, the Northern Kingdom commoner, listening in the town square, must have been feeling rather smug. "That's right, Amos! Give 'em hell! Those heathens and pagans who surround us, those nations whom our Lord will punish, and even those Judean apostates: it's quite right that God should rain down His ire on them!"

But then Amos drops his bombshell: "Thus said the Lord: for three transgressions of *Israel*, for four, I will not revoke it: Because they have sold for silver those whose cause was just, and the needy for a pair of sandals..." The Northern Kingdom listener, lulled into a false sense of complacence by Amos's attack on his neighbors, is suddenly presented with the uncomfortable message of the prophet: Even if those around you are immoral, that does not relieve you of the need to confront your own immorality.

The rest of the book of Amos is an extended diatribe by the prophet: in Israel, against Israel. It doesn't matter what the other nations are doing; it matters what Israel is doing. Verse after verse, page after page, Amos pours out God's wrath against the nation of Israel.

It may be that the ancient commoner listening to Amos was offended, shocked, and outraged by this theological-political message. "We're only doing what everyone else is doing," he might have said. "Are we really that much worse than those around us? Why do we deserve so many column inches compared to the others? What, three lines on Damascus and eight chapters on us? It's such a double standard!"

Amos would not have apologized for this double standard. In perhaps the most famous verse from the book, Amos has God tell the Israelites: "You alone have I singled out of all the families of the earth — that is why I will call you to account for all your iniquities." Being a chosen people comes at a price. The price is that we cannot content ourselves with being the same as our neighbors. We are held to a higher standard.

Amos suggests a different perspective on the double standard of international diplomacy. Is it really acceptable for us to excuse our actions by saying "well, the Saudis do it too"? Is that why we have created a Jewish state here? Is that what we dreamed of for generations? As I suggested earlier in the book, both Heschel and Leibowitz would urge us to answer in the negative. Our mediocrity cannot be justified or excused by the mediocrity of other nations.

One of the reasons for the current existential malaise in Israel may be that we have accepted a vision of Israel as mediocre, as average. It's okay to have Jewish prostitutes because everyone else does. It's okay to have huge gaps between rich and poor because everyone else does. It's okay to use excessive force because everyone else does. But Amos says no. The purpose of our existence is not merely to be no worse than anyone else. We were charged with a bigger goal — that of being a "light for other nations" (as noted several times in Isaiah), a country that others would aspire to emulate. We didn't dream and pray for a return to Zion for two thousand years in order to be average.

I am aware that this approach to Israel's political and economic situation may be utopian and perhaps naïve. We do live in the real world, and that comes with certain costs. As I noted in the previous chapter, on campus and in international diplomacy, we are right to point out manifestations of the double standard and demand that Israel be treated with the same standards as other nations.

But perhaps our ready acceptance of realpolitik has chipped away at something more essential, something more visionary at the core of our national being. Where are our modern day Amoses? Where is the angry internal prophetic wrath? Who is today's Yeshayahu Leibowitz? We have allowed the anti-Semites to dictate our agenda and silence our internal critique. One of the tasks of dialogical Zionism is to enable that prophetic internal critique to rediscover its voice.

Epilogue: Why Israel?

This book has in essence been an extended answer to the most basic and foundational question of the whole field of Israel engagement: why Israel? Why should Israel be important in the first place? Why should we want Diaspora Jews to engage with it? Does it make them better Jews, more complete Jews, happier Jews?

In the past few years, more and more American Jews have been asking the "Why Israel?" question: not "What can we do to support Israel?," nor "How can we teach about Israel?," but "Why should Israel be part of my identity in the first place?" It's not just unaffiliated Jews who are asking this question. I have had conversations with rabbis, rabbinical students, Jewish educators, Jewish communal leaders, and all kinds of other senior and influential agents in the American Jewish community, and many of them are asking the same question.

In thinking about this question, I would like to make a distinction between external diplomacy or advocacy and internal Jewish education. Externally, it's extremely important that we develop a sophisticated and compelling case for the existence of the state of Israel that can hold its own in the arena of international law. In the United Nations, on campus, and in the media, the non-Jewish world must be persuaded that the Jewish people have a right to a nation-state just like all other nation-states. Jewish people of all denominations and nationalities have an important role to play in this endeavor, but it's a role that they are becoming less and less willing or equipped to do.

In the early years of the state, American Jews — and Israeli Jews too, for that matter — could cite a number of clear and compelling foundational needs for Israel's existence, some implicit, some explicit, and these were enough. In the first few decades after the establishment of the state, many of the justifications for Israel's existence centered upon the Holocaust, anti-Semitism, and Arab rejectionism. But as these threats weakened, either because of the passing of time or because of their real or perceived diminishing, the reasons for Israel's existence became less and less convincing. In addition, Israel's actions against the Palestinians, which are often perceived as problematic, embarrassing, or immoral, have have made it even more critical that any discussions, internal or external, begin and end with the continued existence of the state as a fact, not a question.

So American Jews do need to be helped to understand why, from a geo-political perspective, Israel has a right to exist and flourish as any other sovereign nation, and how to communicate this to a wider constituency. But I'm less interested in that external issue; the political scientists, historians, media gurus, communication experts, and international lawyers can deal with it. What bothers me — and what I believe is actually the root issue, of which the external problem is merely a symptom — is the internal problem, and it's that internal problem that this chapter is about.

Recall Alyssa, my student whom I described at the start of this book, who said that she had a perfectly rich Jewish life without Israel. How, in the end, do we answer her?

I believe that engagement with Israel broadens and deepens the perspective about what Judaism is, or what it can be, or what it can speak to. I've touched on this theme many times during the book. Let me pull it together here: Engagement with Israel means that Jewishness is no longer limited to the realms of theology, ritual and prayer. It's not just about what food you eat, or what you do on a Saturday morning. Jewishness becomes something that speaks to the entirety of public civilization. It speaks to what a national healthcare system should look like. It speaks to what a bus system should look like. It speaks to art, to music, to theater. It speaks to how we treat the environment — not just whether our synagogue should have a recycling program, but how a country steeped in Jewish values could respond to the urgent environmental dictates of our time.

Israel demands that Jewishness step up from a local, inward-looking perspective to a national platform. Israel engagement means becoming empowered to enter into complex conversations about what that national platform could be. It means seeing Jewishness not just as the opportunity to derive meaning from certain rituals, but as the invitation to be part of an extraordinary contemporary project. That's why silencing American Jewish critique of Israel is such a foolish educational move: It turns people away from the project. Israel can become a way for American Jews, while remaining immersed in American society, to feel that a relationship with Israel affords them a unique avenue to make an impact on the world.

I think that if Alyssa had been offered a way to engage with Israel through this perspective, she might feel that her full Jewish life could be even more enriched by that kind of engagement. If Todd saw his role as an agent of dialogue with his Israel classmates, he might have felt more empowered to bring his liberal ideas into conversations with them, rather than just stew over his feelings of alienation. If Rachel saw Israel in this way, she'd realize that Israel had enough socks, and that there were more compelling issues in which she could become involved.

And, in conclusion, here's where the give-and-take of a relational or dialogical approach becomes crucial again. Israel needs a larger dose of American Jewishness in order to succeed. At present, Israel's Jewishness is mainly informed by Israeli understandings of Judaism. This has resulted in a national Jewish platform that is much too tribal, too backward-looking. In Israel, where Jews are a majority, where we have power, where we need to figure out how to treat our non-Jewish minorities with respect and equality, we could really do with American Judaism's open-mindedness, tolerance, respect for the other, and generosity of spirit. We need American Jewish creativity and its ability to re-imagine Jewish ritual without fear. American Jewishness could help Israel become a religious civilization that speaks to the outside world, rather than hiding from it.

Dialogical Zionism has the potential to heal both communities. It can help American Jews conceive of their Jewishness in broader and more inspiring ways, and transform the scope of Jewish identity. And American Jewish engagement with Israel can help Israel and Israelis fulfill their potential.

We, the Jewish people, have waited a long time for a moment like this. We have wealth, both financial and cultural; we have freedom; and we finally have a place where we can leverage that wealth and freedom to create a society that is rooted in the best that the Jewish tradition has to offer. We have the technological, educational, and logistical wherewithal for Diaspora Jews and Israelis to work together to make a contribution to the world that is befitting of our 3,000 years of preparation. It's a great opportunity. It would be a shame to waste it.

Notes

Note to the reader: what follows is not a full bibliography or reference list. I've noted here some of the essays, books and articles that are mentioned in the text, for readers who want to explore them further. Wherever possible, I've given resources available over the internet.

Pillar 1: Complexity

For the "Birthright bump," see http://circle.org/israel-poll-data (retrieved 11/15/12)

Cohen and Liebman's piece on the "mobilization" narrative can be found in their essay "Israel and American Jewry in the Twenty-First Century: A Search for New Relationships," in the book *Beyond Survival and Philanthropy*, edited by Allon Gal and Alfred Gottschalk.

The Size Doesn't Matter video can still be found at http://sizedoesntmatter.com/media/videos (retrieved 11/15/12). The factoids can be found throughout the website.

Daniel Gordis's article can be found at http://www.commentarymagazine.com/article/are-young-rabbis-turning-on-israel (retrieved 11/15/12)

Robbie Gringras's essay on hugging and wrestling may be found at http://makomisrael.org/blog/hugging-and-wrestling-2 (retrieved 11/15/12)

Cohen and Kelman's report can be found at http://www.acbp.net/About/PDF/Beyond%20Distancing.pdf (retrieved 11/15/12)

Pillar 2: Conversation

Zakovitch's primary interests are the Bible as literature, the history of beliefs and ideas in the Bible, Biblical historiography, and early Jewish and Christian interpretation of the Bible, and he has published widely on these topics, for the most part in Hebrew. Accessible works by Zakovitch in English include his 1991 book *"And you shall tell your son": the concept of the Exodus in the Bible* (published by Magnes Press, Jerusalem), and his most recent *Jacob: Unexpected Patriarch*, published by Yale University Press.

The citations of Zakovitch's work in this section are mainly translations from some of his Hebrew books and essays, including *David: from Shepherd to Messiah*, his commentary on Ruth, and a little-known essay on the teaching of the Bible from a collection of essays entitled *Mikra V'Chinuch* in 1995, edited by Shammai Glander.

John Dewey's notion of what "educative" means is found in his classic book *Experience and Education* (1938).

Pillar 3: Empowerment

The books by Heschel noted in the text are widely available; the 2nd edition of *Echo of Eternity* is published by Jewish Lights.

The main English text on Leibowitz is a collection of his essays entitled *Judaism, Human Values, and the Jewish State*, ed. Eliezer Goldman (Harvard UP, 1992). In this collection you will find some of Leibowitz's prophetic (in both senses of the term) writings on the Palestinian Territories — for example, his essay "The Territories," pages 223-228 — and also his more complex writings on the relationship between halachah and the state of Israel — for example, his essays "Religious Praxis: The Meaning of Halakhah," pages 3-29, and "The Crisis of Religion in the State of Israel," pages 158-173. See also the important and illuminating discussion of Leibowitz by David Hartman, in his book *Conflicting Visions: Spiritual Possibilities of Modern Israel* (Schocken, 1990), pages 57-82.

An internet-accessible introduction to Leibowitz can be found in a Haaretz newspaper profile of him from 2005: http://www.haaretz.com/prophet-in-his-own-country-1.18564

The article in the Forward by Jay Michaelson can be found at http://forward.com/articles/114180/how-i-m-losing-my-love-for-israel (retrieved 11/15/12).

Nel Noddings's book *Caring: A Feminine Approach to Ethics and Moral Education* was first published in 1984 and released in a second edition by University of California Press in 2003. The citation in the text is taken from a summary of her work on the internet, at http://www.infed.org/biblio/noddings_caring_in_education.htm (retrieved 11/15/12).

Pillar 4: Politics

The article by Joel Westheimer can be found at
http://www.democraticdialogue.com/DDpdfs/PDKWestheimer.pdf
(retrieved 11/15/12).

Shlomo Avineri's op-ed can be found at
http://www.haaretz.com/print-edition/opinion/what-s-happening-to-diaspo-
ra-jews-1.289347
(retrieved 11/20/12).

For an example of Hartman's approach, see
http://www.hartman.org.il/Blogs_View.asp?Article_Id=584&Cat_
Id=273&Cat_Type=blogs
(retrieved 11/20/12).

Complexity Applied: Post-Zionism

This chapter is based on an article I wrote in the journal Conservative Judaism in 2006, entitled "A Conservative Jewish Educational Approach to Post-
Zionism." The essay contains many references to the academic literature, both
Biblical and Post-Zionist, which are discussed in this chapter. In these notes, I
have included only a few of those references, and readers who wish to explore
the issues in more depth are invited to find them in the original article, which
is linked to from my website.

The literature on Biblical criticism and its relationship to Jewish identity
is vast. If you're interested in exploring the issue of Biblical criticism, I would
recommend Richard Elliot Friedman's amazing book *The Bible with Sources Re-
vealed* (2005).

The quote from Driver is from his *Introduction to the Literature of the Old
Testament*, page viii. The quote from Knohl is from his wonderful book *The
Divine Symphony: The Bible's Many Voices*, p. 146. Levenson's quote comes from
The Hebrew Bible, the Old Testament and Historical Criticism, p. 69.

The quote from Zielenziger is from her unpublished dissertation, written at
JTS, "A History of the Bible Program of the Melton Research Center" (1989).

Peter Berger's most accessible book is *The Heretical Imperative* (1980). If
you're willing to brave some harder academic but extremely rewarding writing,
try *The Sacred Canopy* (1967). Gillman's term "master story" comes from his
book *Sacred Fragments* (1990).

The quote from Avi Shlaim is from his book *The Iron Wall: Israel and the Arab
World* (2000), p. 235ff. It should be noted that Shlaim's work has been less well

received than that of many other Postzionist historians. Those who grudgingly respect the scholarship of Morris or Segev argue that Shlaim's work is more tendentious. It is not my job here to comment on the rightness or wrongness of those arguments, but rather to demonstrate the difficulty that Postzionist scholarship in general can create for Zionist collective memory. For a more "traditional" but still nuanced perspective on the build-up to the Six-Day War, see Gershom Gorenberg, *The Accidental Empire: Israel and the Birth of the Settlements, 1967-1977* (2006).

The definition of Post-Zionism comes from an introductory book on the topic by Laurence Silberstein called *The Postzionism Debates* (1999). The Haaretz article on Post-Zionism can be found at http://www.haaretz.com/post-zionism-only-rings-once-1.70170 (retrieved 11/21/12).

Regarding "soft" and "hard" Post-Zionism, my colleague David Mendelsson makes a similar distinction between "radical" and "moderate" post-Zionists. We came to these terms and conclusions independently, and I confess that I find his nomenclature more felicitous, but I have stuck with mine here for the sake of consistency.

The Ilan Pappe quote is from an article called "The Square Circle: The Struggle for Survival of Traditional Zionism," in *The Challenge of Post-Zionism: Alternatives to Israeli Fundamentalist Politics*, ed. Ephraim Nimni (London and New York: Zed Books, 2003), p. 44

For British Masorti/Conservative Jews, any discussion about "what it means to be a Masorti Jew" begins with the writings of Rabbi Dr Louis Jacobs, z"l. Jacobs, more than any other contemporary Conservative thinker, sees the origins/present tension as central to his definition of Judaism. See, for example, his books *Beyond Reasonable Doubt* (London: The Littman Library of Jewish Civilization, 1999) and *We Have Reason to Believe* (London: Vallentine, Mitchell and Co Ltd, 1962). The book by Jonathan Wittenberg noted in the text is *The Three Pillars of Judaism* (1997).

Sarah Tauber's essay on Neil Gillman can be found in the Journal of Jewish Education, 2007, and Gillman's own self-reflective essay can be found in his essay "On the Religious Education of American Rabbis" in his book *Doing Jewish Theology: God, Torah and Israel in Modern Judaism* (2008).

This section of the book emerges from an essay written with Ofra Backenroth and Roberta Bell-Kligler: "Breaking myths, building identity: Practitioner-researcher reflections on running an Israel seminar for Jewish education graduate students," in the *International Journal of Jewish Education Research*, 2010.

Hi Res and Connected

This chapter is based on research that was first published in "A New Heuristic Device for the Analysis of Israel Education: Observations from a Jewish Summer Camp," Journal of Jewish Education, 2009.

What is Israel Education?

The statement from the CIE can be found at
http://www.israeled.org/about.html (retrieved 11/21/12, italics added)

The essay by Reinharz can be found at
https://bir.brandeis.edu/bitstream/handle/10192/22991/
Pres.pdf?sequence=1 (retrieved 11/21/12)

On issues of learning and motivation, a wonderful little and very accessible book is Frank Smith's *The Book of Learning and Forgetting* (1998). The paper by Isa Aron was called "Instruction and Enculturation in Jewish Education," and a somewhat different form of her arguments in it made their way into a book that she co-edited with two other colleagues, *A Congregation of Learners* (1995).

Luntz's booklet can be found at http://www.acbp.net/About/PDF/Report%20-%20Israel%20in%20the%20Age%20of%20Eminem.pdf (retrieved 11/21/12)

The Maxim issue can still be found online at http://www.maxim.com/girls-of-maxim/israeli-defense-forces.

The research project in which the "sales call" rabbi appears can be found at http://www.synagogue3000.org/files/IsraelConversations.pdf (retrieved 11/21/12).

Dialogical Zionism in Practice

Alex Levac's books are:

Eye to Zion (1994); Our Country (2000), available at http://www.amazon.com/Alex-Levac-Photographs-Our-Country/dp/9650510524 (retrieved 11/22/12); and most recently, Israel: the Twenty-first century (2008). They are sometimes hard to track down outside of Israel. Many of his photos can be found on the internet, though.

About the Author

Alex Sinclair is a Jewish educational thinker, teacher and writer. He is the Director of Programs in Israel Education for the Jewish Theological Seminary, and is responsible for creating and directing Kesher Hadash, the Davidson School of JTS's semester-in-Israel program.

He grew up in London, England, and received an MA (Oxon) from Balliol College Oxford. After receiving his PhD in Jewish Education from the Hebrew University of Jerusalem, he was for several years an assistant professor of Jewish education and chair of the education department at the Jewish Theological Seminary.

Since moving back to Israel in 2007, he has taught at the Hartman Institute, the Schechter Institute, and the Hebrew University of Jerusalem. From 2008-2010 he was Director of Research for MAKOM, the Israel Engagement think tank of the Jewish Agency. He has run workshops for adults on Israel education, and also has extensive teaching experience in a wide variety of K-12 contexts, including synagogue school, day school and summer camp. He has published several academic articles on Jewish education and Israel education, as well as opeds in *Haaretz* and the *Jerusalem Post*.

He lives with his family in Modiin, Israel.